MW00748614

ONLY BY
God's Grace

By
Norma
Kennett

TEACH Services, Inc.
P U B L I S H I N G
www.TEACHServices.com ● (800) 367-1844

World rights reserved. This book or any portion thereof may not be copied or
reproduced in any form or manner whatever, except as provided by law,
without the written permission of the publisher, except by a reviewer
who may quote brief passages in a review.

This book was written to provide truthful information in regard to the
subject matter covered. The author assumes full responsibility
for the accuracy of all facts and quotations as cited in this book.
The opinions expressed in this book are the author's personal
views and interpretation of the Bible, Spirit of Prophecy,
and/or contemporary authors and do not necessarily
reflect those of TEACH Services, Inc.

This book is sold with the understanding that the publisher is not engaged
in giving spiritual, legal, medical, or other professional advice.
If authoritative advice is needed, the reader should
seek the counsel of a competent professional.

Copyright © 2013 TEACH Services, Inc.
ISBN-13: 978-1-4796-0126-4 (Paperback)
ISBN-13: 978-1-4796-0127-1 (ePub)
ISBN-13: 978-1-4796-0128-8 (Kindle/Mobi)

Library of Congress Control Number: 2013933474

Published by

TEACH Services, Inc.
P U B L I S H I N G
www.TEACHServices.com • (800) 367-1844

Some names have been changed to protect the privacy of the individuals.

Cover design by Ken McFarland
Cover illustration by Marcus Mashburn
Cover illustration based on the author's dream

Unless otherwise noted, all Scripture quotations are from the New King James Version. Copyright © 1979, 1980, 1982 by Thomas Nelson, Inc. Used by permission. All rights reserved.

Scripture quotations marked NIV are taken from the *Holy Bible, New International Version.* Copyright © 1973, 1978, 1984, 2011 by Biblica, Inc. Used by permission. All rights reserved worldwide.

Scripture quotations marked NLT are taken from the *Holy Bible,* New Living Translation, copyright © 1996, 2004, 2007 by Tyndale House Foundation. Used by permission of Tyndale House Publishers, Inc., Carol Stream, Illinois 60188. All rights reserved.

Dedication

To my daughter, son-in-law, and my two precious grandchildren—my gifts from above.

"Now that I am old and gray, do not abandon me, O God. Let me proclaim your power to this new generation, your mighty miracles to all who come after me."

—Psalm 71:18, NLT

Acknowledgments

To God, for the privilege of being put through the fires of affliction so that I would learn to trust Him with all my heart, and for this I am so grateful. He has equipped me to comfort and encourage others in their despair and hopelessness, placing their hands in His.

I'm also thankful to my family and to the many friends who encouraged me to write this book—and who continually asked if it was finished yet.

To my dearest friend, Mary Morris, whose guidance was a tremendous help during the beginning stages. I appreciated her time, editing skills, and wisdom. Sadly, she has passed away, but she is sleeping in Jesus and awaiting His return.

Pastor Robert and Esme Ross reviewed the book prior to publication and offered valuable suggestions; to both of them, I'm very grateful.

Finally, Ken McFarland faithfully and patiently guided me through the process of editing the book and offered his expertise every step along the way. Knowing he was there to answer my questions and concerns was a comfort.

Table of Contents

Introduction

This little book comes about because of an experience that should have taken my life. As frightening as that was, I consider it a gift from above. When we are suddenly confronted with life and death issues, they quickly direct our thoughts to focus on the real issues of life.

And what are the real issues of life? They include getting to know Jesus, the Lifegiver and Creator of everything that exists. And another is knowing that at any time, you can call on His name, and He is always there, ready to hear your plea.

For these reasons, we are blessed when we are put through the fires of affliction. Count these experiences as blessings, rather than as a hardship or a curse. In Hebrews 13:5, God says, "Never will I leave you; never will I forsake you" (NIV). And in Hebrews 12:6, Jesus tells us, "For whom He loves He chastens." So consider yourself privileged when in despair or overwhelmed. Though the world may seem dark now, endure with His strength and hold on till the storms of this life pass. In looking back, you will see it was well worth having to endure the trials, if that is what it takes to draw you closer to the source of love and mercy and grace.

I pray that you will be blessed and encouraged as you read these pages and discover what God has done in my life. His love for each one of us is more precious than life itself; he proved that by hanging on the cross of Calvary.

"The fact that we are called upon to endure trials shows that the Lord Jesus sees in us something precious which He desires to develop. If He saw in us nothing whereby He might glorify His name, He would not spend time in refining us. He does not cast worthless stones into His furnace" (*Ministry of Healing,* p. 471).

Remember that it's the trials of life that cause us to run to the cross to plead with all our strength for help from our Savior. Remember the promises God has made to His faithful children.

"I go to prepare a place for you, and if I go and prepare a place for you, I will come again and receive you to myself, that where I am, there you may be also" (John 14:2).

He longs to come to this earth and is more eager to take us home to our heavenly mansions than we are ready to go. Can we honestly say that we are one with Him as He is One with the Father? I long for this above all else. Why? Because I have experienced His tender mercies throughout my life, from childhood to full adulthood. We have yet to know how many times we have been protected from harm and were ignorant of the Lord's presence and that of His holy angels.

I pray that my story, my testimony, may encourage you not only to endure trials as they come to you but also to seek God with determination to know Him as fully as possible. Then share your story with others so that they may see God's mighty works and blessings in your life.

We read the following counsel in 1 Peter 3:15: "But sanctify the Lord God in your hearts, and always be ready to give a defense to everyone who asks you a reason for the hope that is in you, with meekness and fear."

Chapter One

An Answer to Prayer

I felt nearly paralyzed with fear. I knew they might find cancer.

During my late thirties, my doctor told me I was a good candidate for breast cancer if I continued drinking or eating anything containing caffeine. Already I was beginning to show signs of abnormal cells.

Back then I enjoyed various delicacies without any cause for concern. Yet every so often, I couldn't seem to help myself and would continue to eat things that contained caffeine. I was playing with fire but figured it wouldn't be harmful because I seldom partook of them.

Now I was in my early fifties, and a day finally came when the doctor recommended that I have my first biopsy. I realized, too late, that I should have listened and taken the warning more seriously. I was so fearful, that my daughter flew from Seattle to be with me. What a blessing that was for me.

Going through this scary experience made it quite easy for me to say no to caffeine in any form. But as the years progressed and the stresses of life took their toll, my annual mammograms began to show more abnormal cells again.

I also lived about ten to fifteen miles from an oil refinery, which at times would spew out toxins and issue a warning to the public to close all doors and windows and to stay indoors for a while.

I thanked God for His guidance in leading me to a friend whose recommendations in turn led me to Dr. Mark Owens. My friend also had gone through something similar in the past, and she highly recommended Dr. Owens. He was one of the most compassionate doctors I had ever met. His kind and soft spirit brought a calmness that assured me that, with his years of experience, I knew I could trust his judgment. Speaking in a serious tone, he explained that during the biopsy, he would take a sample of the abnormal cells and have them examined while I lay on the operating table. And if he found cancer, he would remove the breast at that time. I knew I wasn't the first, nor would I be the last, to experience this dreadful moment. But was I mentally able to handle this? Not really.

I feared the outcome. What would tomorrow bring? In my anxiety, I turned to Jesus, my only source of strength and courage. The night before the biopsy/surgery, I prayed most earnestly: "Lord, I'm so afraid, and I feel so alone. Please be with me in the surgery room. Please guide the hands and mind of the surgeon. And please, Lord, help me *know* while I'm in surgery that You are there with me. I don't know how You're going to do this, but You're God!

You can do anything!"

I had prayed this twice, to be sure God heard me. Adeline, my older sister (the matriarch of the siblings, who lived about two hours from me) was always willing and ready to help whenever help was needed in any way. She agreed to come and spend the night with me so she could drive me home from the hospital and take care of me as long as needed, not knowing how extensive the biopsy might be.

Now, as I met with the doctor the following morning before the biopsy, I again found comfort in his compassion. I felt assured that Jesus would help him do his best. As they wheeled me into the operating room and began giving me the anesthesia, I whispered the same prayer again: that I would *know* that Jesus would be with me during the surgery.

It seemed only moments later that I heard the doctor say, "Norma, surgery went fine. I want to see you in my office Tuesday morning."

It was amazing how clearly I heard him and could remember his instructions despite feeling so groggy.

Then I heard the attending nurse say, "Ms. Kennett, wake up. Wake up!" I must have fallen back into a deep sleep, because I could hardly move or force myself to wake up. It took much effort before I could begin to regain full consciousness.

Then I suddenly remembered! While undergoing surgery I had a dream. Filled with excitement, I tried to tell the nurse that Jesus had answered my prayer and that He was in my dream. At this point, the nurse became a little nervous and asked me to calm down, which was impossible, as I felt exhilarated with joy.

The attending nurse could see that I was no longer under the influence of the anesthesia and was, in fact, quite awake and excited. So he called for another nurse to wheel me to the other recovery room, where my sister was waiting for me. I tried to share my joy with the new nurse as she wheeled the gurney into the elevator, but she didn't know what to make of me. I was bubbling over with enthusiasm as I tried to explain what had just happened. (I'm sure this is not the usual reaction patients have upon awakening from surgery.)

When we reached the recovery room, the doors flew open, and I sat up in the gurney and yelled to my sister, "Adeline, Adeline! Jesus answered my prayer! He was with me in a dream while I was in surgery!" I rushed on, trying to tell her the dream, but she responded by trying to block out her view of me with her outstretched arms.

"You're glowing!" she said. "It looks as if you just came out of a party!"

What? I thought. "No! No! It was Jesus! He answered my prayer—He was with me in surgery in a dream!"

Now, I must and will share my dream, a deeply precious experience.

I dreamed I was sitting across a table from Jesus. I can't remember whether the table was round or square. But His forearms and hands were on the table, with hands clasped together. His head tilted just a bit as He calmly looked toward my chin. I was thrilled and excited at the thought that I was sitting across a table from my Savior. *How can this be?* I wondered. *Am I in heaven?*

As I looked around, all I saw was a vast, open plain with nothing around us. In the far distance, I could faintly see what appeared to be mountains, but it was too far away for me to be sure. It didn't matter, because *I was with Jesus*!

As I sat there across from Jesus, I remember feeling safe, peaceful, so very content and happy. In this calm, happy bliss I looked to my right and noticed that Jesus was also sitting next to me in a chair, without a table between us.

How can this be? I thought. *He's sitting in front of me and next to me at the same time.* His posture beside me was identical to how He sat across the table: His hands folded, but this time on His lap. His head was in the same position as before, looking straight ahead and down a bit. He sat there calmly, as if just waiting ... waiting ... waiting with me in surgery.

Oh, how precious! And oh, how unworthy I felt for such a beautiful answer to prayer.

I felt so invigorated that by this time I was able to dress myself. Upon leaving the hospital, my sister drove us to a Mexican restaurant, where we enjoyed a wonderful lunch together.

My sister stayed with me overnight but left the next day. I was well able to take care of myself and to drive back to the doctor's appointment the following Tuesday morning. The biopsy revealed only precancerous cells. The doctor told me that as long as they stayed precancerous, I would be fine. To this day they have remained the same. *Thank You, Jesus!*

For about a year, I had a clean bill of health and continued quite content with life. But little did I know that I had yet another trial to bear that could prove to be my biggest one yet.

Chapter Two

A Year Later

At the beginning of the following year, I began to notice I was losing the hearing in my right ear. *I guess I'm just getting old,* I thought. But after a while, it began to feel as if something was lodged in my ear. My efforts to flush it out were unsuccessful, so I just tried to ignore the problem for a while.

Until one day, while walking across the parking lot at work, I stooped to pick up a ladybug, lost my balance, and fell to the ground. I tried to get up, but a wave of dizziness washed over me. I sat there dumbfounded, but I finally managed to get up. This had never happened before, so it left me with an uneasy feeling.

My ear continued to concern me. At times, whatever was in my ear seemed to shut out all sound. I also began to lose my balance more often. As this continued, I found myself trying to hold back the panic beginning to build inside me.

Finally, I mustered up my courage and marched off to see my doctor. Without looking in my ear, he said, "I'll have my assistant clean it out; that should help."

For a little while after that, I could hear again, but it didn't last. So I made another appointment. This time, the doctor did look in my ear and told me that it looked as if I had an infection. He said he would send me to an ear, nose, and throat (ENT) specialist who would be able to help me.

The ENT, a kind and gentle doctor, decided that the best thing to do would be to continue the flushing twice a week. That sounded easy enough, but little did I dream that each treatment would cause me to feel as if I was spinning out of control. Each treatment, I held on to the chair with all my might, thinking that for sure I would fly off and land on the floor or be thrown against the wall. When he finished, I felt nauseous and dizzy. The doctor would let me sit still until the room stopped spinning, then help me back to the front desk to set up another appointment.

After twice-weekly visits for some months, I finally asked if a CT scan might help give us a better indication of what might be going on, but he said it would be too expensive. Even though I told him that I had great insurance, he insisted that we wait.

Finally, a friend suggested I try charcoal poultices each night. I had never heard of this treatment before, but she carefully showed me how to apply a poultice on my ear. Each night I faithfully followed her instructions while continuing to go in for the flushing treatments.

Two weeks went by. At the next appointment, the doctor looked into my ear and, quite startled, asked, "What are you doing?"

"Nothing!" I replied (I was afraid to tell him about the charcoal poultices for fear he would suggest that I was causing the problem by applying them). Using an instrument, he took something out of my ear that looked like a small brown scab. He put it into a small plastic container to send to the lab for a biopsy. When the report came back, I was relieved that it was not cancer.

But the pattern continued—with poultices each night and flushing twice a week—and more brown material continued to work its way out of my ear. Another biopsy also brought a negative report, and all the while, something in my ear seemed to open and shut at different times.

Finally, things took a very different turn. The doctor looked alarmed and told me I needed to get a CT scan *right away*! When I asked him if he would set up the appointment, he said "No"! Yet he insisted I must do it right away. I felt overwhelmed because now I knew for certain that something must be very wrong.

About 4:30 in the afternoon, I left his office. As soon as I got to my car, I prayed that by God's grace I would be able to book an appointment right away. As I sat there, I could feel my heart racing and a surge of panic beginning to envelop me. I called the number the doctor had given me and waited. A woman answered, and I explained the problem.

"We don't have anything available at this time," she said, "but I think I can get you in about three weeks from now."

My heart sank.

"Are you sure?" I responded.

"Yes, I'm sure" she said.

"Would you please check your schedule again?" I persisted. "It's very urgent that I have an appointment right away."

She reluctantly agreed but said, "I'll look again, but I don't think that will do any good." I continued to pray that by God's grace He would provide an opening for me. It seemed as if I waited a long time. When she returned to the phone, she said, "This is your lucky day! Can you come in tomorrow morning at 11:30?"

"Yes!" I almost shouted. "I'll be there!"

Another answer to prayer! The next morning I was there with time to spare. In no time at all the procedure was over. I was so grateful and relieved to have the CT in one day.

Little did I know that it wouldn't be long before I would be facing another major surprise.

Chapter Three

Emergency Room Visit

Late the next evening following the CT scan, I was lying in bed, unable to sleep and feeling very restless. I felt pressure building in my right ear. When I pressed on my ear, fluid ran down my neck and onto my pillow. Immediately, the room began to spin. I grabbed hold of the headboard, afraid I might black out or faint. Breaking into a drenching sweat, I felt weak and as if I were about to lose all my bodily fluids. And mentally, I was spinning out of control.

I was able to crawl to the bathroom, then crawled back and onto my bed. Lying there short of breath, I felt I was about to die. I pleaded with God to sustain me until morning.

Whom can I call at 1:30 in the morning? I thought. The name of a friend who might be able to help came to mind, even though she lived quite a distance away. But I could only remember the area code and the first three digits of her phone number. Suddenly, I saw the remaining four numbers in red in the darkness. *Strange,* I thought. *Why are they in red?*

Ever so slowly, I struggled to make my way across the bed to the phone. All the while the room felt as if it were still spinning. I left a message asking her for help and to call me as soon as possible.

Eventually, the room stopped spinning, and I was able to rest in peace as I continued talking to Jesus, asking again and again that He would sustain me till morning. I was so afraid that if I happened to fall asleep, I might not wake up.

Morning found me rested. I believe the Lord allowed me to sleep awhile, yet I was still weak and drenched but not quite so dizzy. I slowly reached across the bed for the phone and called my friend again. This time she answered, saying she had just turned her phone on but had not yet had a chance to check her messages. I explained the situation and asked if she could take me to the emergency room. She agreed to come as soon as she could pack her things.

I lay there for about an hour and a half until I heard the front door open as she let herself in. By God's grace, I had loaned her the key to my condo because she would stay at my home one night a week while attending a chaplaincy class near my home. I thanked God that she was able to open the door on her own.

Quickly, she climbed the stairs, but when she reached the bedroom doorway, she just stood there staring at me, with her mouth open.

"I'm not taking you anywhere!" she finally said.

"Why?" I asked.

"I'm afraid you'll pass out before we get there! You're white as a ghost, and you look awful!" I tried to reason with her, but she insisted I call my doctor first and handed me the phone. When I reached the doctor on call and explained what had happened, he OK'd the trip and told me to tell them, when I arrived, that my doctor said he thought I'd had a ministroke. Woe!

Not surprisingly, the ER was crowded. Still weak and lightheaded, I, with my friend's help, managed to work my way slowly to the front desk. However, the receptionist didn't pay any attention to the message from the doctor and indicated that we would have to wait our turn. I was in no condition to convince him otherwise at this point. We had barely worked our way back to our seats, though, when the receptionist told us we were next on the list. Another prayer had been answered.

I was wheeled to a room and given a gown and a bed. Soon I was taken for another CT scan. When the attendant returned with the report, his eyes were big as saucers as he said, "Lady! You need to see a doctor! You have a large mass in your head."

Stunned and almost speechless, I whispered, "What? A large mass? Are you sure?"

"Yes!" he repeated. "You need to see a doctor right away. You have a large mass in your head."

I asked for the scan, but they refused to release it. I felt numb and somewhat paralyzed. My mind raced, trying to take it in. I knew things were bad but never imagined it would be this bad. I had never felt pain, just the annoyance of a little door in my ear opening and shutting, along with the dizziness.

I was in a state of shock as my friend helped me back to her car, drove me home, and stayed with me that night. The next day I called the lab, explained the situation, and was able to make arrangements for my friend to pick up the earlier CT scan that had been taken just a few days prior, so she could take it to my doctor. When the doctor saw the scan, he asked her to bring me to the office right away.

When I arrived, he seemed to be in a state of shock. He said I needed surgery immediately but that he would not be the doctor to perform it. He told me I needed to see Dr. Kevin McKennan. He had his assistant call to set up an appointment. She returned in a few minutes with the news that Dr. McKennan was on vacation for two weeks.

On hearing this news, I froze. Then the doctor said, "Go home and call Dr. McKennan's office every day until you can get an appointment." He gave me my CT scans and sent me home.

Two weeks seemed like a lifetime. Would God keep me and help me hold out till then?

Chapter Four

The Waiting

For the next two weeks, I was in a state of anxiety and foreboding.

I felt so alone. I called my employer and explained that I would be off work for an indefinite period of time. My days were spent calling Dr. McKennan's office, hoping against hope that he would be back before my condition worsened. I even tried calling other doctors, thinking they might be able to help me sooner, but I quickly learned that being a new patient would mean a longer waiting period to get in. Still, I went ahead and made a few appointments anyway. It just seemed to help knowing that if one couldn't help me, I would have a backup.

I struggled with losing my balance and at times found myself having to crawl up the stairs, holding on to whatever would support me as I tried to move around. Mostly, I just rested and prayed that my heavenly Father would sustain me until the doctor returned.

Every night I'd ask God to keep me awake through the night for fear I wouldn't wake up. And I prayed that He would support me and sustain me so that I could see another sunrise, another sunset. I could feel the presence of death very near. It felt as if a dark, heavy shadow was following me everywhere I went. Death felt so close that I feared if I were to stop suddenly, it would overtake me.

One morning John, a friend from work, called to see how I was doing. When I explained the situation, he startled me by saying, "The devil is after you! I'll call you back."

Before long he called and gave me the number of a doctor in Placerville. "Call him right away and see if you can get in today," he said. "I'll come by and take you there myself."

I called immediately, and they set up an appointment for one o'clock that afternoon. John picked me up, and we arrived with plenty of time to fill out the paperwork.

As soon as I was called, I handed the doctor my CT scans, and he began to study them. Quite a few pictures had been taken, so he took a while to respond. Finally, he agreed I needed surgery right away but told me he was not qualified to do it. He was sorry he couldn't help me, and then he asked me who my doctor was.

I told him about Dr. McKennan and the others I had called, whereupon he asked his assistant to get a background check on each of these doctors. It didn't take long before she returned with the information. He quickly read through it and said, "Wait for Dr. McKennan."

My sister was waiting for me when I got home.

She also had a key to my home and had come to see how I was getting along.

"Oh, by the way," she said. "You got a call from Dr. McKennan's office. They want you to call them right away to set up an appointment."

My spirits soared, then soared even higher when I called and learned that Dr. McKennan was back and wanted to see me first thing in the morning. Surely, my prayers were answered, and I praised God for taking care of me.

My sister left, as another friend called from work to see how I was doing. I explained I finally had an appointment. She volunteered to take me to my appointment in the morning. Oh, how I thanked God for providing family and friends who would take time away from work to help me in my distress!

I was excited and concerned, as I wondered what the doctor would say and how that would change my future.

Chapter Five

The Doctor's Appointment

"I know all about you!" Dr. McKennan greeted me the next morning with his arm stretched out and pointing directly at me. "Dr. Mackry and I have been emailing each other while I was on vacation." Praise the Lord! It was such sweet music to my ears to hear that the process had already begun. "Let me have a look at your CT scans."

After Dr. McKennan had looked them over carefully, he said, "We will do surgery tomorrow. There is a possibility that afterward you may have a permanent tick on the right side of your face, or it might even be paralyzed. And you may never taste food again."

"What time will you perform the surgery?" I asked. (Shocking as his comments were, something even more important was on my mind.)

"I don't know," he replied. "I just got back, and my schedule is full. Maybe 5:30, 6:00, or 7:00 in the evening sometime."

"How long will it take?" I asked.

"That depends on what I find. It could take four or five hours or more."

I began to put it all together. Tomorrow would be Friday. The days were shorter in March. I knew it got dark early. But all I could hear were the words of the fourth commandment in my mind: "Remember the Sabbath day, to keep it holy. Six days you shall labor and do all your work, but the seventh day is the Sabbath of the Lord your God. In it you shall do no work: you, nor your son, nor your daughter, nor your male servant, nor your female servant, nor your cattle, nor your stranger who is within your gates. For in six days the Lord made the heavens and the earth, the sea, and all that is in them, and rested the seventh day. Therefore the Lord blessed the Sabbath day and hallowed it" (Exod. 20:8–11).

I was filled with anguish, and tears began to well up in my eyes. I was afraid I might begin sobbing. So I turned to my friend Denise, who had brought me to my appointment, and mouthed the word *Sabbath*, for I feared that if I spoke at this moment, I would lose control and sob out loud. Then I turned toward the doctor.

"What? Are you crying?" Dr. McKennan asked sympathetically when he saw my tears. I turned toward my friend with a gesture as if to say, "I can't speak."

"It's her Sabbath," she explained.

"What?" he asked with a puzzled look on his face.

By God's grace, I was able to speak at this point. I

spoke up and said, "It's the Sabbath of the Lord God. I can't have surgery on the Sabbath day." I went on to explain that Sabbath begins at sunset on Friday and ends at sunset on Saturday.

He was astonished, as if in disbelief, then paused for a moment, and said sympathetically, "Norma! You're *not going to make it* till Monday."

I nodded and said, "I know, but I'm not going to make it if I don't have peace."

He said something to the effect of "I don't believe this!" He just looked at me and shook his head. "I'll see what I can do to rearrange my schedule," he said, "but I can't promise you anything. My assistant is making an appointment for you to get an MRI today. Get the MRI, wait for it, then return it to me before the day is over. I need to see it before surgery.... Then go home," he continued, "and get your papers in order. I'm not sure you are going to make it through the night or through surgery tomorrow."

I walked out of his office numb and in a daze, but by God's grace, I did as I was instructed. My MRI appointment was at 3:00 that afternoon. It was still early, so we stopped at Sacramento Central Seventh-day Adventist Church and found Pastor White in his office. I told him my story and asked if he would anoint me, which he graciously agreed to do. Afterward, we all prayed, and I felt at peace. This proved to be a balm to my soul.

Denise and I stopped for lunch. But because I was in a constant state of dizziness and feeling a little nauseous, and also going through mental and emotional trauma, I could hardly eat. After lunch we continued on our way to the lab for the MRI.

I was unprepared for the strange, repetitious knocking sounds during the MRI procedure, but I was able to focus my thoughts on various Bible verses and began to sing hymns in my mind. The Lord felt very near to me, and I was much calmer.

After the MRI was finished, we had to wait quite a while for the results. Finally, they gave me a large, heavy-duty manila envelope, and we headed back to the doctor's office. We arrived shortly after closing, but they were waiting for us. The doctor thanked me for the MRI, and we headed home.

The day wasn't over yet. In between lunch and the MRI appointment, I had called work to bring them up to date. I asked to talk with John Bridges, who worked in the Planned Giving department at Amazing Facts, where I worked at the time, to see if he would come to my home that night to help me write out my Last Will and Testament. He agreed to be there about 7:00 that evening. My sister Adeline again agreed to come and stay so she could take me to the hospital the next day in case I could be scheduled early in the day.

As Denise drove me home, I felt numb inside. Was this really happening to me? We talked about the possibility that maybe, because we had prayed and I was anointed, the mass would be gone and there would be no need of surgery. But that wasn't the case.

All the while, I was holding on to the hand of faith, knowing that Jesus was with me and was walking beside me through this cloud of dread. An inner strength and calmness kept me going. At the same time, I had a very real awareness of the moment that this was not a dream.

Yet I knew that Jesus was near and that He would stay with me through what was yet ahead.

Chapter Six

A Time of Prayer and Confession

When we arrived home, my sister was already there, ready to do whatever was needed to help me get through what lay ahead. Soon John Bridges and his wife, Tama Jo, walked in, sharing hugs and showing expressions of concern. He prayed before we began, and then he and I sat at the dining room table as my sister and Tama Jo talked quietly in the living room. John handed me a pen and told me what to write:

"I, Norma Kennett, being of sound mind, do declare this to be my Last Will and Testament ..."

God, by His grace, gave me the inner strength and clearness of mind to write these words and to complete what needed to be affirmed, should my life end. To have this settled and complete was gratifying. In my life I had never thought of this moment before, yet it arrived in one day. When the document was finished, my sister signed on the witness line, and John went to make copies. When everything was completed, I thanked John and Tama

Jo for their kindness in assisting me through this process.

Later, while getting ready for bed, I wondered if this would be the last time I would ever go through the ritual of flossing, brushing my teeth, and washing my face. Kneeling by my bed, I prayed for my family, beginning with my daughter, son-in-law, and my precious grandchildren. I pled that God would save them for eternity. Then I continued with my dad and my siblings and their families (my mom had passed away the year before, and in my heart I knew she would be in the first resurrection). Finally, I prayed that God would arrange things so I could have my surgery early in the day to give the doctor enough time to finish before the Sabbath began.

Then words driven on a tidal wave of anguished emotions came rushing out of my mouth: "Lord! I didn't think I would die of a tumor! I thought my blood would be used for "seed in the last days!" (The early church father Tertullian wrote that "the blood of the martyrs is the seed of the Church.") I prayed the way I did because I'd had three dreams in my adult life in which I was being persecuted for my faith. However, I realized that no matter what my lot was to be, it was more important to cling to the assurance that my Lord and Savior has already walked that path, and He has promised He will walk it with me, holding my hand: "Lo, I am with you always, even to the end of the age" (Matt. 28:20).

As soon as I had finished speaking to the Lord, a light flashed across my mind. I understood this light to represent my life—and it seemed so small!

"Lord!" I cried out. "You know my life from beginning to end! You know that if I should live, I might do something foolish and lose my salvation. Oh, no, Lord! Not my will, but Thy will be done! Just help me remember everything I have not confessed. I need to be assured before I get off my knees tonight that if I should die tonight or tomorrow, I will be in the first resurrection."

I confessed to God on a daily basis, but given the reality of the moment, it seemed possible that this could be my last request ever. For me, there was no promise of tomorrow. So I anxiously remained silent, waiting and waiting. But nothing.

"Lord!" I repeated, please reveal any unconfessed sins. I will not get up off my knees tonight unless I *know* for certain that I will be in the first resurrection." In time, a few things came to mind. Relieved that the Lord heard me, I said, "Yes, Father! Forgive me. What else, Lord? What else?" I waited patiently, as time seemed to stand still. But in those fleeting, agonizing moments, nothing came to mind.

I continued to plead: "What else, Lord?" Then another impression came to my mind. "Yes, Lord! I'm sorry; forgive me, Father. More, Lord! What else? 'I will not let Thee go unless Thou bless me.'" Again, I waited on the Lord to reveal anything that would keep me from the first resurrection and eternal life with Jesus.

Suddenly, a gentle sense of peace and God's presence came over me, a peace only God can supply. The peace that surpasses all understanding washed over my soul. A weighty burden had been lifted from my shoulders. I felt that I was the happiest woman on earth. I knew at that moment that there was nothing between my soul and my Savior. (These words reminded me of a song with this title, but now it had so much more meaning than ever before. I consider it one of my favorites.) Being fully surrendered to God is an amazingly beautiful and peaceful state of mind that cannot be fully described with words.

That night I slept like a baby, with a constant smile on my face. Even though I didn't know whether I would ever wake up again, it didn't matter because I knew that if I was to die that night, I would see the face of Jesus at the last trumpet call of God. This thought filled me with incredible joy and peace. It no longer mattered what would happen. *Take my life, take my home; my stuff has no hold on me. Nothing matters but Jesus.* What a beautiful place to be—at rest in the arms of my Savior.

Tomorrow, maybe surgery or maybe not. But tonight, peace.

Chapter Seven

The Morning

Morning came, and much to my surprise, I woke up. I was still here!

I thanked God for another day and reminded Him that another "bridge" remained to be crossed but that I knew we would cross it together.

At 9:00 a.m. Dr. McKennan's assistant called to tell me that the doctor had been able to rearrange the schedule. She told me to be there at 10:30 and that the surgery was scheduled for 12:30. Amen! With a grateful heart, I thanked God for the precious soul who gave up their surgery time for me.

As we drove to the hospital, I couldn't help but think about how—even three to four weeks earlier—things had "worked together for good" long before I knew it. I had gone to my primary care doctor because I just didn't feel well. He had ordered blood work and an EKG. Little did I realize at the time that these would be needed for my present surgery. The Lord was way ahead of me.

"It shall come to pass that before they call, I will answer; and while they are still speaking, I will hear" (Isa. 65:24).

On our arrival at the hospital, I found my friend Silvia waiting for me. She was truly concerned for me and had come so she could pray with me before the surgery. I smiled to myself and told her that all my papers were in order and that I had prayed for all my family members. I was in perfect peace because there was nothing between my soul and my Savior. She said she would continue to pray for me, and I thanked her for that. Then I said goodbye to my sister, and she assured me she would be in the waiting room.

Soon, I was wheeled to the room where my doctor was waiting. He came over to see how I was holding up. I was OK whatever happened; I was ready. I said goodbye once more to my sister. From there, they rolled me into the operating room.

Only God knew the future from here. I was completely in His will.

Would the doctor be able to finish the surgery by the time Sabbath began? Would I survive? I wouldn't have long to find out.

Chapter Eight

That Night

I woke up from surgery about 8:30 that evening. Once again I was surprised and relieved to find that I was still here. I thanked God for His amazing love, grace, and mercy, and for allowing me to continue on.

"Lord," I said, "You must have a purpose for me. I don't know what it is, but I surrender my all to You this night. All my life I have lived for myself; now I am wholly Thine. Wherever You want me to go, I will go; whatever You want me to do, I will do; and whatever You want me to say, I will say, for I am wholly Thine!"

Tears ran down my face, and my grateful heart seemed to grow larger by the minute as I once more surrendered my future to God, however long that future would be.

Soon a nurse walked into the dark room to check on me. I asked her what time my surgery had ended. She said she thought it was sometime between 4:30 and 5:30. Glory, hallelujah—we had kept the Sabbath!

The next day Dr. McKennan came by to see how I was getting along. He explained what he had done and mentioned how glad he was that the surgery had started as early as it did, because it was very long and intense. He wasn't sure he would have been able to be so technical and precise later in the afternoon after a full day of surgeries. Praise the Lord for His mercies.

My tumor had a name: a *cholesteatoma*. Kind of like a little Pac-Man, a *cholesteatoma* conquers and destroys as it devours especially bone, muscle, and other tissue, which is exactly what it did in my case.

The tumor had worked its way into my brain a full inch, and this was Dr. McKennan's chief concern. He thought I could die if it were to puncture the thin membrane in the *dura* area, located right behind the ear. This keeps the liquid in our brain, and he feared that I could die of spinal meningitis.

Dr. McKennan continued to explain how he had cut behind my right ear, top to bottom, laid it on my face, and then began to remove the tumor, being careful not to puncture the thin membrane, which by this time was stretched very thin. The tumor had managed to consume all my hearing bones, except for leaving a fragment of my balance bone.

"I drilled a section of your skull," he said, "and removed the bone. I pulverized the bone to a powder, then added glue, and made a bone pâté. I used the fragment of your balance bone, combined it with the sculptured bone, and attached it to your right skull."

Why there? Because there was nothing left to attach it to behind the ear; that was all gone.

My surgeon then cut a section of the soft bone tissue covering the skull and placed it over the dura area for better reinforcement. He finished by sewing my ear back where it belonged. Whew! I was glad I slept through the whole thing.

Throughout my stay at the hospital, I was blessed with visits from my sister, friends, and from Pastor Thompson and his wife, Helen. But now I was eager to get home!

Oh, what joy and gladness I felt for the blessing of life and for a wonderful doctor who was able to help me when others couldn't. This was yet another gift from God.

Chapter Nine

Going Home

After a couple of days in the hospital, I was released, and my sister drove me home. I lived alone, due to my divorce, yet was blessed with my family and friends, who were always there to help. We had made arrangements for my daughter to come and stay with me a few days, if I survived. Just as Adeline and I were saying goodbye, I saw my daughter drive into the complex. I can't describe the joy that filled my heart to see her once more. Our plan was that she would take care of me for about three days after the surgery. She wanted to come sooner, but my grandson was still so small that I felt more at peace having him with his mother.

The next three days were special. Each moment was priceless. Our roles were reversed. My daughter was now taking care of me, and I enjoyed every minute of it. Our time together was more lovely and comforting than I had ever imagined it could be, a precious gift of time and togetherness. It was just what I needed. The worst was behind me, and now I had the freedom just to enjoy my family.

But all too soon, it was time for my daughter to

leave. Oh, how I dreaded to see her go. But I thanked
God for her and for all her help and the tender, loving care she showed me while tending to my needs.
I also thanked Him for all the prayers on my behalf
by her church family and for my son-in-law, as he
stayed home to take care of my grandson, who was
still quite young. By God's grace, I would now have
the opportunity to live to, and beyond, the age of 60
and have the opportunity to be a grandmother a little longer.

I remained home for two months, and during
that time I continued to receive get-well cards, phone
calls from far and near, flowers, and homemade
soups from fellow coworkers. In addition, and much
to my surprise, the employees from Amazing Facts
sacrificed a day's wages for me so that I could continue to support myself during the recovery. This was
above and beyond the call of duty, and it touched
me so deeply that it brought tears to my eyes; it still
does each time I think about it. It's hard to describe
the love I felt from family and friends and coworkers.

Chapter Ten

A Voice in the Night

I was welcomed back to work on a half-day basis, until I was strong enough to work full-time again. During this time I had a strange and wonderful experience. One night I lay in bed reading the chapter on the crucifixion of Christ in *The Desire of Ages.*

Out of nowhere I heard a voice say, "Norma!" I knew I was home alone, so it startled me. This brought back the memory of a time soon after my mom had died. It was her voice that I heard calling my name in that certain way that only she could. I knew immediately it was an evil spirit, because the Bible tells us the dead know not anything (they are unaware of anything and thus can't speak, and they remain in their graves until the resurrection). I was reminded of Ecclesiastes 9:5 that tells us, "For the living know that they will die; but the dead know nothing." And 1 Thessalonians 4:16 that says, "For the Lord Himself will descend from heaven with a shout, with the voice of an archangel and with the trumpet of God, and the dead in Christ will rise first."

So in my mind, I asked Jesus to remove this evil spirit from my room, never to return again. Then I began to hum the children's tune of "Jesus loves me, this I know" over and over again, until everything became peaceful.

Now here I was again, a year later and a voice was saying, "Norma!" So in my mind, I asked, "Is that You, Lord? I'm confused and afraid to answer."

Then the Voice said, "Norma, do you remember the dream you had a year ago in surgery?"

"Yes, Lord!" I replied.

"The time I sat across the table from you," the voice continued, "was for the times I took the place of your father, who was never home for you as a child."

My thoughts went racing back through my early childhood preschool and kindergarten years through first grade, remembering how often I had longed to be with my earthly father. His work kept him away for a month at a time. Then he would come home for just one night before leaving again for another long month. While he was home, I would cling to him till it was time to be put to bed. The next morning I would hold on to him for dear life as I watched my mother pack his suitcase. All too soon he would kiss us all goodbye, then get into his car and drive away. I would stand at the window until the car disappeared from sight and cry for hours, hoping he would return. I did this day after day. Whenever my mom told me to get away from the window, I would sob, "No! I want my daddy."

Throughout my childhood, sadness would sometimes overwhelm me. I'd weep and not know why. I would ask my mom, "Why do I feel so sad?"

"I don't know, my child," she would answer. Years later she told me that she feared I would die of a broken heart because I couldn't be comforted.

Now, in my late fifties, my heavenly Father was telling me He had been there with me all along the way, from my earliest years even until now. His words went straight to my heart. I sat up in bed, trying to taking it all in, and an incredible joy began to well up inside me. I felt as if I were about to burst out laughing. But before I could, He continued.

"And when I sat next to you without a table between us, that was for the times I took the place of the husbands who were never a husband to you."

As I began to understand the full meaning of these words, I thought my heart would burst, and I was filled with an abounding love that overwhelmed me to sobs and tears of gratitude.

I thought of my marriages. Glen and I were married maybe a year and a half. He spent most of that time with his parents. He finally told me his mother was the most important woman in his life.

Bob and I were married seven and a half years. I didn't want to see the end coming, but it was there.

William and I were married twenty years, eighteen of which were very difficult. When things got just too emotionally painful, he agreed to get counseling. On the first visit, the counselor advised me to leave him, but I hung in there, hoping things would improve. But in time, it was obvious things would always be the same.

Toward the end of this marriage, I went to three different pastors for help, to know if I should leave. Each one said the same thing: "Norma, he left you a long time ago." In my heart I had known this was true, but I needed to hear it from others.

So when the Lord told me that He had taken the place of the husbands who had never been husbands to me, I began to weep from the depths of my soul as I felt my heart filling up and spilling over with an incredible joy I can't describe. One minute I was laughing and the next I was sobbing. I was overcome with a joy beyond measure. For the first time, I felt completely loved, safe, and whole. Words really can't express what Jesus did for me at that moment in time.

I continued to laugh and cry for some time. I thought that if anyone were to find me in this state of mind and emotions, they would surely call the medics and take me away!

After a while I calmed down. Then I got on my knees next to my bed, and with tears still running down my face, I prayed, "Lord! I don't want this moment to end." Jesus felt so near, and I wanted to savor the moment a little longer. The thought that it would end was unbearable.

Lord, I continued in my silent prayer, *I wish this moment would last forever. I don't want You to leave, but I know You're busy and You have lots to do. But I would like to ask for a miracle. I will ask it in my mind, as I don't want the evil one to hear me and try to deceive me with a false miracle. Lord, please show me a pure, white dove, so that when I see it, I will know it's You. I know You're always with me, now more than ever before. But to see something tangible, to be able to reach out and almost touch it—oh, Father, that would be so precious, so wonderful!* I prayed this twice to seal my prayer.

I climbed back onto the bed but was unable to continue reading. I had, just moments ago, felt so close to the Savior I was just reading about. So I just lay there reliving this amazing experience that had transformed my life and presented me with a grander picture of the God of Heaven than I had ever known until now.

Would the Lord grant me a miracle so amazing as the one I had just asked of Him? Was I being presumptuous even to ask?

Chapter Eleven

A Miracle

Every day I would casually glance around, hoping I would see a white dove. I thought to myself, *It would be all right if I didn't see one,* but deep down in my soul was the longing for such a personal confirmation of my experience. Another day went by and no dove. One week, then two, ...

At the end of the second week, I was sitting in church enjoying the Sabbath school lesson taught by Pastor Doug Batchelor. That Sabbath an academy graduation was scheduled to take place along with the sermon, but since I did not know any of the graduates, I decided to go home and spend special time with my heavenly Father in quiet study and prayer. I got in my car and proceeded toward Highway 50, heading east.

As I drove over the overpass, came around the curve that leads onto the freeway, and began to come out from under the shadow of the overpass, something caught my eye. I quickly looked to the right and saw the most beautiful, brilliant white dove heading toward me. It seemed to be just waiting for me there—it almost took my breath away.

At first I thought *No!* Then *Yes! No? Yes!* I was in and out of disbelief. Then I realized, *Yes! This is the dove for which I prayed!* In amazement, I looked at it, wide-eyed, wishing I could let go of the steering wheel and force my eyelids to open even larger with my hands so I could get a closer look. Just then, time and space went into another dimension.

What took place next, I can't tell you whether it lasted a few minutes or a split second. Everything went into slow motion, and my eyes seemed to turn into zoom lenses. The dove was so close that, were it not for the windshield, I could have touched it. As it flew in closer, I could see its beautiful wings gracefully moving up and down in slow motion.

As it reached just about the middle of the car, I saw its wings extend upward, and as my eyes zoomed in, I could see every minute detail of every feather. I could see how beautifully the dove's feathers rested, one on top of the other and next to one another. I felt as if I were directly under its wings. The sight before me was most beautiful.

Psalm 91:4 then came to mind: "He shall cover you with His feathers, and under His wings you shall take refuge." I was awed by the sight before me, or, should I say, above me. This was an amazing moment. Then the wings gracefully and gently came down. And when the dove was directly in front of me, in my mind I heard a voice ask, *Can you see Me?*

Yes, Lord! I see You!

Instantly, the dove disappeared, and suddenly, everything returned to normal. I found myself driving down the freeway, yet I couldn't tell if I had covered any distance. Immediately, I remembered the Bible story of Philip baptizing the Ethiopian in the River Jordan, and how, before the Ethiopian came up out of the water, Philip disappeared (see Acts 8:38–40).

So I continued on my way, weeping tears of joy and calling out to my Savior, "Lord! You laid the foundation of the earth and stretched out the heavens!" (see Isa. 48:13). "Yet You still took time to hear a small child's prayer!" The chariot that was my Toyota Camry continued down the freeway as I rejoiced all the way home. What a never-to-be-forgotten experience!

Chapter Twelve

The Movie

All my life, I knew there was a God, but in my childhood, He seemed to me bigger than life and far, far away somewhere in heaven. I had a general idea of what He looked like from the pictures I saw, mostly of Him hanging on a cross. Seeing Him hanging there like that made me sad. I never knew why or what it really meant. All I knew was that I needed to confess my sins if I did something wrong.

When I was about 17, my boyfriend took me to a movie in San Francisco. I lived in the Bay Area at the time, and driving to San Francisco for a movie was especially exciting. This would be the first time I would see a movie on a wide screen called Cinemascope, the latest invention in the movie industry back then.

The movie was called *The Greatest Story Ever Told*. As you can guess, it was about the life of Jesus. The images on this enormous screen were spectacular. The music was lovely, and the scenery was breathtaking.

For the first time, I began to get a real picture of who God was, in human form—in His Son, Jesus Christ, who hung on the cross. I observed Christ's baptism and heard the voice of God say, "This is my beloved Son, in whom I am well pleased."

I witnessed Christ calling the twelve and noticed how they loved Him and hung on His every word. I saw His compassion as He healed the sick and raised the dead, something I had never imagined. I marveled as He multiplied the loaves and fishes to feed thousands. I was warmed and delighted as Jesus rode into Jerusalem on the donkey, with all the people shouting hosannas. I was amazed as He walked on water and showed His power to calm the raging storm.

Then I watched Jesus break bread with the disciples at His last meal on earth, which explained the meaning of the pictures of the Last Supper my mom had in our kitchen all those years. Soon after, I was appalled when I saw one of His own, one He did not call but who had joined in among them, betray Him for thirty pieces of silver. Next, I was stunned and horrified as the mob yelled "Crucify Him! Crucify Him!" I couldn't comprehend how their hatred could descend to this despicable level.

In shock I watched as they beat Him and whipped Him and shoved the crown of thorns upon His head and treated Him with the most disturbing kinds of cruelty. I felt sick to my very soul. And at the same time, I was awestruck at how He remained calm refrained from saying a word. Then I was overwhelmed when they placed the cross on His shoulders and He began to stagger and fall. I felt I could stand no more. But when they nailed Him to the cross, my heart sank and felt as if it were breaking into a million pieces.

I began to sob almost uncontrollably, yet as quietly as I could. I was shocked and offended. This was more than I could bear. Then I heard Him pray for His persecutors, saying, "Father, forgive them, for they do not know what they do" (Luke 23:34). I wondered how He could utter such words after they had so brutally assaulted Him in their evil rage. This cruelty displayed toward the innocent Son of God was beyond my comprehension, so I put my head down and felt I could watch no more. Finally, I looked up, to see Jesus rising higher and higher toward heaven.

When we walked out of the theater, I couldn't speak; I felt numb to the bone. I felt I would cry uncontrollably if I tried to say anything. Neither of us spoke. As we got into the car and began to drive across the Bay Bridge toward home, all I could say was "I didn't know, I didn't know, I didn't know" as I struggled all the way home to hold back the tears. My poor boyfriend just remained quiet. I believe it could have been his first understanding of the real picture of good and evil and of the debt that was paid for our sinful souls. Or maybe he just didn't know what to do with his emotionally devastated girlfriend.

This was the first time I was introduced to my Lord Jesus Christ, who is now my Life and my All. The book of Isaiah shares this with us about Jesus:

"He is despised and rejected by men, a Man of sorrows and acquainted with grief. And we hid, as it were, our faces from Him; He was despised, and we did not esteem Him. Surely He has borne our griefs And carried our sorrows; Yet we esteemed Him stricken, Smitten by God, and afflicted. But He was wounded for our transgressions, He was bruised for our iniquities; the chastisement for our peace was upon Him, and by His stripes we are healed.... He was oppressed and He was afflicted, yet He opened not His mouth; He was led as a lamb to the slaughter, and as a sheep before its shearers is silent, so He opened not His mouth" (Isa. 53:3–7).

What amazing love! What an amazing sacrifice for a sinful world, for you and for me! This is beyond human understanding.

A favorite hymn of mine is "When I Survey the Wondrous Cross." Every verse is beautiful, but one line in particular always reaches deep into my heart:

"See, from His head, His hands, His feet, Sorrow and Love flow mingled down. Did e'er such love and sorrow meet, Or thorns compose so rich a crown."

The last part of the last verse reads:

"Love so amazing, so divine, demands my soul, my life my all."

The Bible assures how us how strong this love is. "For God so loved the world that He gave His only begotten Son, that whoever believes in Him should not perish but have everlasting life" (John 3:16).

"Paul saw that the character of Christ must be understood before men could love Him or view the cross with the eye of faith. Here must begin that study which shall be the science and the song of the redeemed through all eternity. In the light of the cross alone can the true value of the human soul be estimated" (*The Acts of the Apostles,* p. 273).

Yes, friends, the greatest story ever told is the story of Jesus. And will be throughout eternity.

Chapter Thirteen

Heavenly Music

Bob and I, it was obvious, were heading toward separation or divorce. Our daughter was only three years old, and the thought of a divorce horrified me, as it would cause her emotional trauma not to have her daddy around (I knew only too well from my own childhood how painful that felt). He was still living with us, but it was getting pretty uncomfortable for both of us.

One night, as he lay on the outer edge of his side of the king-sized bed, and I was far over on the other side of the bed, my mind raced, wondering what was to become of our family. The room was dark and quiet. In the distance I could hear a faint sound, but I couldn't tell exactly what it was. I thought to myself,

What is that? Maybe the neighbors listening to music? Hmmm. It sounds like music, but different. Is it singing? No. Maybe instruments? The sound was faint and hard to distinguish.

I had to know, so I said, "Bob?" No response. A little louder: "Bob! Are you sleeping?"

"What!" he replied, startled.

"Do you hear music?"

"No, I don't hear anything."

For a while it was quiet again. But in a little while, I heard it again. I still couldn't figure out if what I was hearing was singing or instruments, but it was so beautiful. Never had I heard anything quite this beautiful before. Once more I asked, "Bob, do you hear it now?"

"What? No! I don't hear anything."

Why can't he hear it? I thought. *He's closer to the window than I am.* I believed it must have been coming from near the window. Again it became quiet and still. But in a short while, that beautiful sound was back. I decided to just be still and listen. I felt calm and peaceful, as if I might just float away on a cloud and disappear into nothing. The sound was heavenly.

Then it dawned on me: *Could this be angels? Am I dying? Is that what's happening? It's too beautiful to be anything else!* My heart began to race. *Oh, that must be it!*

"God!" I prayed. "Please don't let me die. My daughter is only three years old, and I know no one can love her as much I do. I'm her mother. Please, Lord!"

In earnest I prayed, fearing I might not have an opportunity to finish rearing my own daughter. In the midst of my confusion, I realized it was quiet again. Finally, in a stressful state, I fell asleep.

Now, as I look back many years later, it seems that the Lord was with me through that painful experience. He knows our every fear and heart's cry.

And I believe in my heart of hearts that He was allowing me to sense a little of the peace of heaven in the midst of the storm and trials of the painful divorce that lay just ahead.

Just as Jesus calmed the storm on the Sea of Galilee, He is also able to calm your heart and soul and mine through the storms of this life.

"He who spoke peace to the billows of Galilee has spoken the word of peace for every soul. However fierce the tempest, those who turn to Jesus with the cry "Lord, save us" will find deliverance. His grace, which reconciles the soul to God, quiets the strife of human passion, and in his love the heart is at rest. Ellen G. White says, "He maketh the storm a calm, so that the waves thereof are still. Then are they glad because they be quiet; so he bringeth them unto their desired haven" ("Accepted in the Beloved," *Review and Herald,* October 15, 1908).

Chapter Fourteen

Reading the Bible

In the process leading up to our divorce, Bob moved out into the guest room. This was a difficult time for me, because I had my three-year-old daughter to provide for, and I also needed to begin thinking about getting the house ready to put on the market so we could divide the proceeds and begin our new, separate lives.

As I shared in my earlier testimony, I again couldn't be comforted. But this time, I couldn't eat and couldn't feel the ground under my feet. I felt I was in a daze. All colors faded from sight; all I could see were tones of gray, black, and white. To work was difficult; it took much effort to concentrate on anything. So I began to run. I ran every day to help me feel again. A sitter would come and watch my daughter as I ran three miles each day.

Then I remembered that I had the Bible my mother-in-law had given me for Christmas a year earlier. I remember kneeling by the side of my bed. This now felt unfamiliar to me, as I had lost what I had discovered when I saw the movie *The Greatest Story Ever Told* many years earlier. Life got in the way after that, and other things had taken first place above my Lord. So now I was in desperate need of real comfort. Nothing, and no one, could help me. The things of this world lost their flavor. I was broken and empty.

So I placed the Bible on my bed, knelt next to it, and said, "Lord, if You're real, I need to feel Your presence." That's how far I had strayed from the Lord—that I felt I needed to use the word *if.* "I don't know if I can read all the words or pronounce all the names, but I need to feel Your presence." I continued. "I have never read the Bible before—this will be my first." Then I got into bed and began to read, from 9:00 p.m. until 3:00 a.m. I can't explain it, but I was not able to put the Bible down. Finally, I went to sleep.

The next morning I got up at 6:30, got my daughter ready for preschool, dropped her off, and then drove myself to work. Each day this was my routine. When I got home, the babysitter would come and watch my daughter, I'd run three miles, and then my daughter and I would have our special time together and get ready for the next day. Each night I'd sing to her before I turned off the lights, but I left the door open in case my daughter were to call me in the night.

On my knees each night, I would ask the same thing, with my Bible on the bed: "Lord, if You're real, I need to feel Your presence." And every night, I'd read from 9:00 p.m. to 3:00 a.m. This went on for six months. During this time period I survived on three and a half hours of sleep, ran three miles a day, worked eight hours a day, and took care of my daughter. This could only be accomplished by God's grace, strength, and a thirst for His words of life.

Like the woman at the well, I was feeding on the Bread of life and drinking from the well that shall never run dry. And through the Holy Scriptures, I was filled until I could take no more as I became immersed in the warmth of God's love.

By the end of these six months, I had reached the book of Revelation. I had been transformed from a woman who couldn't be comforted to a woman who thought she would literally burst and explode from the love that swelled within her. I'll try to explain.

Picture in your mind a midnight-black room, where you're not able even to see your hand in front of your face. Then you notice a bright beam of light, brighter than the sun and about the width of a strand of hair, in the middle of the room. And as you watch, it begins to widen, until the brightness becomes unbearable because you fear the brightness of the light will consume you.

Now, exchange the light for love. That's sort of how much love I was experiencing. It felt as if, were I to receive just one more ray of light, one more ounce of His love, I'd explode like a balloon. So I prayed a prayer I now wish I hadn't prayed. I prayed that God would not love me so much, because I didn't know how to contain more. There was no more room in my soul; it was full and overflowing.

"Why are you crying?" my mother asked me. "Is it the divorce?"

"No, Mama, it's because Jesus loves me."

She looked puzzled, then said, "Tell me how this is."

"Mama," I told her, "it's not like when a parent loves a child, it's not like when a husband loves a wife, it's not even an infatuation—it's not physical."

"No?" she replied.

"No, Mama, it's millions of miles above the heavens. It's hard to explain. It's unlike anything I have ever known. There is no language that can describe it in words. It's bigger and better than love on earth. It's incomprehensible to me."

Friends, we will have to wait until Jesus comes in all His glory for that moment when we will be changed from mortality to immortality (1 Cor. 15:53). But before this, we can begin to have a little understanding of the love that comes from heaven. The Bible declares that "Eye has not seen, nor ear heard, nor have entered into the heart of man the things which God has prepared for those who love Him" (1 Cor. 2:9).

Chapter Fifteen

The Restaurant

By the time Bob and I were at the point of "thinking of divorce more seriously," he was still living in the guest room. I was reading my Bible six hours every night, still thinking there was hope for us. So I called him at work and said, "When you get home tonight, let's go out to dinner. I have to talk to you." I had already made arrangements for a babysitter, so he agreed to keep the dinner date.

We went to a restaurant in Danville, close to where we lived. When we walked in, I noticed it was dark, illumined only by the candlelight on each table. The place was busy, so we waited for our name to be called. My heart was sure I could explain a way out of a divorce. As we waited in this dimly lit room, I turned to look at the people having dinner. I can't explain what came over me, but as I watched them, I was overcome by an incredible love for each one. I didn't know who they were. Some of them would glance in my direction as they talked with their friends; others, I could see only their backs or their sides. All I knew was that I was overwhelmed with love for people I didn't even know.

After our name was called, we sat and talked. But nothing I said made a difference. I guess I was making a last-ditch effort to save what was about to be lost. Finally, I was able to accept the situation.

However, since that time I've had a similar feeling come over me—an overwhelming love for the people I just happen to be with at the time and an abundance of joy in those moments! I just so wish it could be there all the time. I'm sure heaven will be far beyond what I felt in that restaurant, though. There we'll all love one another with a love we have not yet experienced or can even imagine. Earthly love is fleeting, but heavenly love will be eternal. I long for that day; don't you?

"Behold, I am the Lord, the God of all flesh. Is there anything too hard for Me?" (Jer. 32:27). No, my friends, nothing is too hard for Him. He can transform us and change our hearts if we let Him. With God all things truly *are* possible.

Chapter Sixteen

A Dream in Danville

Along with my routine of reading the Bible six hours every night, I also began to have dreams and experience unusual occurrences, all good ones. One night I had a dream, and looking back, I'd say it probably occurred because of a certain Bible chapter I had previously read. But I'll share it just the same.

That night I dreamed I was driving down a frontage road not too far from where I lived. Because it was about midnight, few cars were on the road. I noticed that up ahead, a four-car pileup had occurred. Mine was the first car to arrive from the north side of the accident. It looked as if the four cars had all come from different directions at high speeds, ending up at an intersection at the same time—a sight to behold, for sure. On impact, all four cars ended with their hoods up in the air, leaving only their back tires on the ground, with fire around them. Think of how elephants in a circus position themselves in a circle facing one another, front legs raised, while standing on their hind legs. That's how this looked, except for the fire all around the cars.

All around at the scene in this dream were police and other people, and I wondered where all these people had come from at such a late hour. Sitting in the car, I thought of how dreadful this was and prayed there would be survivors.

Then I looked in the rearview mirror to see if any cars were behind me, but what I saw took me by surprise. I saw Jesus sitting in the back seat! In the rearview mirror, I could see His eyes looking at me. They seemed to be telling me that I should drive into the fire. My eyes were glued to the rearview mirror as I asked, in my mind, *You want me to drive forward into the fire?* He nodded yes. I did as He requested and soon found myself sitting in my car, surrounded by the flames of the accident. Yet I saw that Jesus was still with me, still sitting in the back seat. I had no fear, only peace, because He was with me.

Maybe the reason I had this dream was that I had just read the story of the three young Hebrew men thrown into the fire as written in the book of Daniel. I can't say for sure if that was why, but most probably.

Thinking back on that dream, I know that if a day should ever come that I would be persecuted for my faith, I would pray that I could look and see Jesus— just as He stood with the three Hebrews—standing with me. And if not, then by faith I would pray that I be enabled to endure whatever might come to me.

We have this promise that, "When you pass through the waters, I will be with you; and through the rivers, they shall not overflow you. When you walk through the fire, you shall not be burned, nor shall the flame scorch you" (Isa. 43:2).

What a powerful Bible text! What a reminder that no matter how bad things get, Jesus is there!

Chapter Seventeen

Falling From the Roof

My divorce with Bob was traumatic for our daughter and me, but it was especially hard on our daughter, who was three years old at the time. When she realized that Daddy was sleeping in the guest room, she questioned why. I explained that we were not getting along. She said, "Mommy, you have to learn how to cooperate!" Her words were spoken with such determination that it took me by surprise, and I was filled with sadness.

Then one day after Bob had come home from work, we were talking in the kitchen when our daughter went behind him and pushed him toward me, saying, "Daddy, kiss Mommy. You never kiss Mommy anymore." It was heart-wrenching to know that the tender heart and mind of our child could sense the void in our home.

After Bob moved out, we sold the house, and I purchased a home in another town. It was there that I met William who was divorced from his wife but had no children. We became friends. Our friendship lasted for four years, at which time we were married. It was a blessing to have a father in the house again.

My husband William and I decided to roof our house. He requested that the roofers remove the old layer of composition paper that had accumulated over the years and deliver new roofing materials and supplies onto the roof. William's idea was that we would install the roof ourselves. The roofers did a really nice job clearing the roof down to the bare wood and placing all the materials we would need on the roof. We were ready to begin with a clean slate, but the night before we were to begin, it rained. We thought we had planned well, because this was the middle of July, yet it rained anyway, right on the bare wood.

Early the next morning, William went in search of a hardware store that might be open. After a while he returned with a load of clear plastic and began to cover the roof. It continued to rain for a while, then eased up.

"Come up and help me cover the rest of the roof with the plastic I brought," he said. I climbed up the ladder from the back of the house, as he instructed, and walked toward the front of the house, heading to the chimney, where he was. The plastic was very wet, so I was cautious as I walked to the other side. Nonetheless, I began to feel myself slipping and heading toward the edge. So I lay down with my hands in front of me and stopped at the ledge. The gutters held me in check.

Stunned, relieved, and a bit breathless, I laid there, unable to move for a minute or two. Then I carefully sat up and walked slowly toward the back of the house to let myself down the ladder.

"Come back and help me," William said. But I refused. All I wanted to do was get off that roof!

I headed toward the back of the house as he proceeded to urge me to come back to where he was so I could help him. I stopped and thought about it, and in time, I worked my way back to where he was. I had planned to walk in a different direction, but he insisted I take the same way as before. But again I began to slip toward the edge of the roof, sliding down head first with my hands in front of me.

This time, I slid right on past the gutters and over the edge head first. Something was happening in mid-air. I could feel my body turning so that I was in a sort of sideways sitting position. If you can imagine a leaf falling from a tree as it blows back and forth in the wind, I felt the same, coming down gently to the ground.

When I landed, I marveled to see that I had settled safely, just missing the concrete walkway and the rose bush we had just trimmed. The fall did knock the wind out of me, and I sat there for a while gasping for air and realizing that an angel must have broken my fall and situated me just so, to miss all that would have harmed me.

It could have been much worse than having the wind knocked out of me. My back was out of adjustment, and in time a chiropractor was able to realigned my back. My husband insisted I return to the roof, but I decided to take a break and make breakfast. In a while the sun came out, and we began the process of removing the plastic from the roof so we could begin laying down the black tar paper as the base for the shingles. We completed the work in two and a half weeks, including adding on two skylights.

How often are we put in dreadful and dangerous situations, and how often can we look back to see that, by the grace of God, He has brought help to rescue us? It's true we don't always walk away unscathed. And sometimes it's our own fault; sometimes, not.

I'm reminded of some wonderful Bible promises: "For He shall give His angels charge over you, to keep you in all your ways. In their hands they shall bear you up, lest you dash your foot against a stone" (Ps. 91:11, 12).

"The angel of the Lord encamps all around those who fear Him, and delivers them" (Ps. 34:7).

"Our help is in the name of the Lord, who made heaven and earth" (Ps. 124:8). Amen!

Chapter Eighteen

Afterthoughts from the Drive to Rio

Thirteen years had passed since Bob and I divorced, and now we were both remarried. My daughter was now sixteen and attending a Christian boarding school, Rio Lindo Academy, as the Christian high school in our town only went through the tenth grade. I'll never forget a conversation we had one weekend as I drove her back to school, about an hour and a half away. On this Sunday morning, we had just stopped for a bite to eat, then continued our drive.

Out of the blue, she said, "Mama, I know the divorce with Daddy was hard on us, but if that's what it took for us to find our church and for me to have Christian teachers and Christian friends, then, Mama, it was worth it."

I continued driving, with tears rolling down my face, as I listened to my young daughter speaking these precious words. God sometimes gives young people words of wisdom far beyond their years. I agreed with her 100 percent. She had put it all together in a single sentence.

So every time we come to a place in our lives that seems unbearable and ask ourselves, *Why me? Why now?* just remember that we never know what God has in store for us up ahead. Looking back, I see what could have happened had we stayed in the town where we lived while I was still married to her father and where my daughter would have continued her education. Very possibly, she could have grown up in a quite different environment and with a very different attitude on life. It was a wealthy neighborhood, and I heard that many of the children who grew up there had wild parties and did all kinds of crazy things. I thank God that we moved and found a Church with beautiful brothers and sisters in the faith. I don't question God as before but only trust Him, as only He knows best.

At thirty-eight years of age, I made my decision to completely and fully trust my all to Jesus. This was two years after my marriage to William. Because of the invitation of a neighbor, I attended the last seven meetings of a Revelation seminar and realized that Jesus had been wooing me throughout the years. At times I came very close to making a full commitment, but every time, I let something or someone take His place.

I actually felt He would not accept me now and felt it was too late for me, but through my tears, my pastor assured me that Jesus was still waiting with open arms and that it was up to me to decide. He also made it clear that I had not committed the unpardonable sin. In this church I learned many truths about what living a Christian life really meant.

I felt honored knowing that Jesus, in spite of all my past sins, would still love and accept me. I learned that being baptized meant that all my sins were buried and washed away in a watery grave. I was baptized, against my husband's will. He threatened me and ordered me not to go through with it, but I was hearing another voice now.

However, this caused a division between William and me because we were no longer equally yoked. At first he felt cheated, feeling that I loved Jesus more than him because I no longer enjoyed the things we use to do together, like going to jazz clubs. Now I enjoyed quiet time reading my Bible and Ellen White's writings. As a family we still enjoyed going to the zoo and museums and engaging in other family outings, but things felt different. There seemed to be a constant battle in our relationship that could never be settled. We tried counseling, but nothing changed.

I began to see a change in his attitude toward me. He would speak harsh, hurtful words that would sometimes make me cry. Then he would say, "Go ahead and cry; I have no sympathy for you!" If we went anywhere, he would walk ten feet ahead, and he always appeared angry.

One day I felt I had had enough verbal abuse. After arguing over nothing, I left the kitchen and ran to the bedroom where I sobbed and cried out, "Lord! What am I to do?" I didn't want my daughter to experience another divorce and go through the pain of having another father leave. As I sat on the bed rocking back in forth in my anguish, pleading for some wisdom, I suddenly heard a loud voice in my head that said, "Love ... him ... more." These words were spoken slowly, loudly, and firmly. I stopped crying. Having never heard this Voice before, I remained silent. In a little while I timidly said, "Is that You, God?" Silence ... I thought, it must be God, because the evil one only speaks of hate and getting even, but God always speaks of love and forgiveness, so I felt it must be God. Assuring myself that this was in fact my Savior, I then had the confidence to say, "Then you'll have to put that love in my heart because I have nothing but contempt for that man!"

Again I heard Him say, "You know My love, but William doesn't." It struck me that our Father knows every minute detail of our lives. Suddenly I sensed an amazing peace flood my soul. This was the first time I had heard my Lord's voice and felt the peace of the Holy Spirit.

Taking a deep breath and wiping away the tears, I thanked my heavenly Father for hearing and answering my prayer, showering me with His peace and filling my heart with His love to equip me for this crisis. What a relief! The burden and heaviness in my heart completely melted away. I marched myself back into the kitchen where William was still standing, and I said, "Ten minutes ago I was ready to ask you to leave this house until you could treat me with some decency." I continued, "I know you don't believe in God, but as I was crying, asking God what I should do about us, He said to love you more."

At that point William replied by making a scary ghostly sound. "Ooooo, now you're hearing voices. You're crazy!"

Calmly I replied, "No! I'm not crazy. I'm going to be a better wife, more patient and loving." At this point he walked away.

I believe God asked me to love William more to give him an opportunity to come to know the Lord. It was by God's love and His Holy Spirit that I was able to do my best to show William Christ's love, patience, and forgiveness. It was not my strength but His Holy Spirit that kept me strong and calm. To God be the glory! When humanity and divinity work together, amazing things can be accomplished.

For a while there was a glimmer of hope. Over time William began to recognize that maybe there was a God. He even purchased a small paperback book of the four Gospels. And he began to ask questions, such as why did Jesus ask the disciples not to tell others about His miracles. His heart began to soften, letting rays of heavenly light into his understanding.

At one point William even attended an evangelistic meeting with me one night that was held at my church. William struggled with the ideas that were presented because they were contrary to his evolutionist way of thinking. For a while he seemed to embrace the message, but sadly his interest didn't last long. The world and his profession continued to lure him back.

Today, I am now a new creation in Christ Jesus. I am married, in a sense, to my Jesus. I reflected on His goodness, in that He died for me, even though I was still a sinner. No greater love exists than giving up one's life for another. Jesus gave His life for me, so how could I not consider giving it back to Him? I felt I could willingly die for my Savior.

I discovered, to my delight, the unique relationship and joy the seventh-day Sabbath brings to my life. John 1:3 reminds me that Jesus is the Creator of everything that was made, including the Sabbath. He blessed this day, decidedly setting it apart from any other day of the week so we can spend special quality time just with Him and have time to joyfully reflect on His goodness. Sabbath is a unique time of closeness intended for all of God's children, a time that's ours to develop a relationship with Him and continue growing to be like Him and become one with Him. I have confidence, knowing I can always call on Him for help in every situation.

His ten commandments have become so clear and real to me, protecting me and giving me wisdom to make right choices. God's law is His personal handwritten love letter straight from His heart to ours, a personal letter inscribed in stone for all who will receive it and obey Him in love.

"The law of God is as sacred as God Himself. It is a revelation of His will, a transcript of His character, the expression of divine love and wisdom" (*Patriarchs and Prophets*, p. 52).

I was amazed to learn that eating a healthy

diet according to the guidelines He has given in the Scriptures could give me a better opportunity to hear His voice, live a healthier life, and sustain me through the difficulties of life. And oh, how this would indeed sustain me through the difficulties I faced! I'm so grateful to Jesus for helping me along the way, for I sense that I would have perished had I not had the hope of a blessed Savior.

Trials strengthened my faith in my Savior. I thank Him for every one of them. These trials have assured me of just how near He is and have banished all my fear that He would ever forsake His children. He left the ninety-nine sheep to go find that one lost sheep (soul). I was one of those sheep who was lost, then found. I'm sure there are many out there who, like the prodigal son, are longing for a father who is patiently awaiting and searching for his son to return to His loving arms. The prodigal received this certainty when he returned feeling totally unworthy and yet received his father's love and acceptance. Aren't these stories profoundly wonderful in reminding us, in word pictures, of the unspeakable love of God that patiently and persistently waits those for whom He died and gave His all? He could do nothing more for us, as He completely emptied Himself for us. Again I understood that although I am not worthy, His worthiness covers me by His love and His blood.

I had a sign in my cubicle when I worked at Amazing Facts that read: "Don't worry about tomorrow; God is already there!" And He is!

The apostle Paul says, "And we know that all things work together for good to those who love God, to those who are the called according to His purpose" (Rom. 8:28)!

Ellen G. White keenly states, "If received in faith, the trial that seems so bitter and hard to bear will prove a blessing. The cruel blow that blights the joys of earth will be a means of turning our eyes to heaven. How many there are who would never have known Jesus had not sorrow led them to seek comfort in Him" (*Thoughts From the Mount of Blessing,* p. 10).

"God has a purpose in sending trial to His children. He never leads them otherwise than they would choose to be led if they could see the end from the beginning, and discern the glory of the purpose that they are fulfilling" (*Prophets and Kings,* p. 578).

This has been very true for me. It's when we hit rock bottom that we find there is nowhere else to look but up.

Chapter Nineteen

A Dream in My Apartment

William and I tried our best for eighteen years after my baptism. There were happy times, but we could never come to any agreement. So, after almost twenty years of marriage, we separated for a while, and about a year later, I filed for divorce.

The Lord bears long with His children, but He never forces His love upon us if we are not willing to receive it. I was very discouraged and cried often. I stopped going to church because I would embarrass myself when I couldn't hold back the tears of sadness and would have to leave in the middle of the service. One Sabbath morning I woke up after having a vivid dream. In it I was still living in the Bay Area. I had been invited to what seemed like a party at a condominium not far from where I used to live. These condos were still brand new when I moved away and had not yet been occupied. But in my dream, I'd been invited to a function in one of them.

Many people were there. The women were wearing cocktail dresses and held wine glasses in their hands while talking and laughing in little groups. I felt out of place, as my dress was plain and simple. Looking around, I realized I didn't recognize anyone and felt very much alone. So I walked out on the front porch, which faced north. Now it was early evening, and my eyes were drawn toward the sky, which was unusually beautiful. I couldn't remember ever seeing it this lovely before.

The sky was somewhere between a brilliant royal and navy blue. And throughout the heavens, I could see stars glistening like brilliant diamonds. They were all uniformly larger than usual, yet strangely, the distance appeared the same between each of them. As I stood there in awe, gazing at this amazing sight and taking in the beauty of the heavens, I was lost in the wonder of it all.

Hearing an unexpected burst of laughter, I turned to look back inside and found that it came from a group of four, specifically, from two couples I'd seen visiting together earlier. Then suddenly, I heard a loud, thunderous sonic boom that shook the earth. When I turned and looked up to the sky again, I was astounded at what I saw. It was as if something had punctured a hole through the atmosphere and left a huge, wide, gaping hole. In the middle of this opening, I could see what looked like liquid fire in all sorts of beautiful colors. It moved and churned as if it were an angry ocean. The outer edges curled out as if they had been torn open, and they, too, were alive with liquid fire. However the rest of the sky surrounding this great opening was as before, still and calm in a canopy of brilliant deep blues and laced with those unusual large stars throughout.

I stood there, fearful, wondering if this could be a warning that Jesus was about to come. I thought to myself, *Am I ready? Is my heart clean and pure, without spots or wrinkles as the Bible describes? Am I worthy to see Jesus and live? Should I—or would I—run from the brightness of His coming to the rocks and cry out for them to fall on me?* The Bible says those not ready for Christ's return will do this.

I'd been depressed and couldn't quite tear myself loose from the pity party I was having because of my divorce. But now I wondered if I was really ready to face eternity. It was time to get on with my life and get closer to the only One who truly loved me and could save me.

I turned to see the reaction of the others to what I'd seen in the sky but was amazed to find that all were calm, as if nothing had happened. *Nobody noticed? Hadn't they heard the thunderous sound and felt the ground shake?* I wondered. *Doesn't anybody care or even know that Jesus could come, and we're not ready?*

When I looked back toward the sky, the hole was still open, yet the inside was calm, with its brilliant, beautiful blue hue. The stars were still in the heavens but not in the center of the wide, gaping hole. All the heavens surrounding the opening appeared as calm and beautiful as before, leaving only the outer edges still on fire and in a rage of movement.

I believe this dream was a wake-up call for me. I had taken my eyes off Jesus, lost faith, stopped going to church, and no longer spent time in God's Word as before. But by God's grace, He got my attention through the amazing dream, which opened my understanding to see the seriousness of the moment. The Bible tells us that in the last days "men [and women, too!] will dream dreams" (Joel 2:28).

Any day could be our last; we just never know. Every day we wake up is another chance to get it right. I pray that none will be caught off guard by His appearing. The time we have left must be spent wisely, getting to personally know the Savior for ourselves and getting fortified by the Word of God so we may be able to stand with peace as we face the storms just ahead.

The Scriptures describe the climactic scene of Christ's return:

Then the sky receded as a scroll when it is rolled up, and every mountain and island were moved out of its place. And the kings of the earth, the great men, the rich men, the commanders, the mighty men, every slave and every free man, hid themselves in the caves and in the rocks of the mountains, and said to the mountains and rocks, "Fall on us and hide us from the face of Him who sits on the throne and from the wrath of the Lamb! For the great day of His wrath has come, and who is able to stand? (Rev. 6:14–17)

Again, in Paul's epistle to the Thessalonians, we read, "For the Lord Himself will descend from heaven with a shout, with the voice of an archangel, and with the trumpet of God. And the dead in Christ will rise first" (1 Thess. 4:16).

The apostle warns: "For you yourselves know perfectly that the day of the Lord so comes as a thief in the night. For when they say, 'Peace and safety!' then sudden destruction comes upon them, as labor pains upon a pregnant woman. And they shall not escape.... Therefore let us not sleep, as others do, but let us watch and be sober" (1 Thess. 5:2, 3, 6).

Ellen White wrote, "Every act casts its weight into the scale that determines life's victory or defeat. And the reward given to those who win will be in proportion to the energy and earnestness with which they have striven" (*The Acts of the Apostles*, pp. 313, 314).

And King Solomon, the wisest man to ever live, wrote this, "Let us hear the conclusion of the whole matter: fear God and keep His commandments, for this is man's all. For God will bring every word into judgment, including every secret thing, whether good or evil" (Eccles. 12:13, 14).

I'm glad to know that as long as there is breath in us the Lord will continue working for our present and eternal good. Jesus is our only hope whereby we can be free from sin and eternal damnation: "Acquaint yourself with Him, and be at peace" (Job 22:21). Amen!

Chapter Twenty

Ski Lift

When William and I had been separated for quite a few months, I still hadn't filed for divorce. It was winter, and I decided I wanted to learn to snow ski. In my youth I'd had a little experience, but too many years had passed since then. After taking a few lessons and driving myself to the smaller ski resorts, I felt it was time to buy my own equipment so I could afford to ski more often.

As a child William had learned to ski quite well, and now he could ski KT22 in Squaw Valley with ease. I was finally graduating from the bunny hill to intermediate. I was happy and enjoying the ease of perfecting my turns as I skied downhill, and at those times it almost felt like a graceful ballet.

Our separation had not left us with hateful feelings toward one another; in fact, we became better friends than we were when living together as husband and wife. We would talk on the phone from time to time, and I shared with him my enjoyment of my new love for winter skiing.

"Why didn't you tell me you like to ski?" he asked.

He must have forgotten how, every year, I would

suggest we go snow skiing, but he always refused. Anyway, we decided we would spend a ski day together. We went to a nearby small ski resort and had a great time. So we then scheduled another ski date. But this time he suggested we try a larger ski resort, such as Squaw Valley. *Gulp,* I thought, *that's pretty steep.* It was here that the 1960 Winter Olympics were held in Squaw Valley and KT22 ski run was where some of the downhill races were held. But he assured me that they had easy runs there, too. I agreed to try, but I had a bad feeling about this.

When we arrived, he went to KT22, while I found a softer and gentler intermediate slope. When we met for lunch, he suggested we try another run that he thought I could handle. I began to feel uneasy, just as I had felt on occasions when we were married and he decided we should do something that seemed always to turn out to be not in my best interest. Again, after much urging, I finally gave in and said, "I'll try it." He convinced me it was not difficult at all, and I sort of believed him. We put on our skis and skied over to several different chair lifts in order to get to the one he had in mind. Finally, we arrived at the slope he had picked for us. As we approached the lift, I noticed it only seated two people.

He got in first and reached his arm over to my side of the bar and held on tight. So when I went to sit down, I struggled to find room on the seat, as his arm was in the way. I somehow found an edge barely hanging on with my bottom but was not able to hold on to the bar, which was behind me. We were climbing higher every minute.

I told him to let go of the bar so I could scoot back on the seat, but when I looked into his eyes, they had turned from brown to black, and it seemed as if he were looking right through me. I tried to break his hold on the bar, but he wouldn't budge. I kept trying to talk with him, but he just stared at me stone cold and didn't react to anything I said as if he couldn't hear me. Higher and higher we went, and I could feel myself slipping off what little space I had. I tried several times to break his hold, but he just stared at me as if he weren't even there.

I prayed most earnestly, pleading with God to help me break William's strong hold, because I felt I was about to slip off the chair. By God's grace, He kept me balanced as I gave one last desperate shove with my elbow and finally broke William's hold. I quickly grabbed for the pole and scooted back all the way into the seat. I was pretty distraught, to say the least, while trying to catch my breath.

"What are you doing?" I asked him. Then, to my dismay, I heard a gravelly voice say, "I'm being cuddly."

"Who *are* you?" I replied in my distress. But he just stared ahead, not answering. When we approached the top of the mountain, he jumped off the chairlift and skied down the hill by himself. When I jumped off the chair, I skied forward and discovered I was on a black diamond run; the sign was staring me in the face.

The top of the hill looked like the top of a bald head. There was nowhere to go but almost straight down. *I did it again,* I thought to myself. *I allowed him to talk me into a dangerous situation.* I continued to feel that this was not going to end well. I surveyed the mountain and saw a place that looked a little less steep, where I could zigzag down the mountain.

As I got halfway down the hill, I heard a whistle—William's familiar way of trying to get my attention. From where he was, he motioned for me to follow him. I stopped where I was and shook my head NO! But then I realized his route was the only way down from where I was. I kept my distance and followed him over to the other chairlift to work our way back to the starting point.

I thank God the other chairlifts were large and seated more skiers. We eventually found a way to get where the gondola was located. I wanted desperately to get on the gondola so I could rest all the way down, but it wasn't stopping for anyone. It was late and just about closing time, so everyone seemed to be rushing to get on this one path that led to the main buildings below.

By this time my legs felt weak as wet noodles. I had no strength to get down this icy, slippery ski run without crashing into something. Everyone was skiing so fast. A snowboarder jumped over a high spot and hit me as I tried to keep up with the crowd to keep from getting run over. Thank God, I didn't fall. It felt as if we had been skiing for about twenty minutes. The run was a very long one, and I thought we would never reach the bottom.

Suddenly, we came to a place where people were jumping onto another downhill slope, but I was going so fast I missed it. I could hear William yelling from behind me, "Why didn't you follow the rest of the crowd?" I saw that the path ahead of me would soon run out of snow, as I could see patches of dirt here and there, and eventually, all dirt. So I decided to just sit on my skis. By this time only a few of us were on this path. It seems we had all missed the turnoff.

Finally, I stopped just before the snow ran out. Physically and mentally exhausted, I felt relieved as I just sat there, unable to move. My legs were shaky and weak. William was right behind me, a bit upset with me and wondering what on earth I was doing.

I slowly took off my skis, gave him the skis and poles, and told him to take them, because I intended to walk the rest of the way. He jumped onto the downhill slope and skied to the bottom. I took my time and realized I needed to file for a divorce right away. This episode had pretty much sealed the deal.

I thanked my heavenly Father again for rescuing me from another disaster, for breaking the hold that could have taken my life had I completely slipped off the ski chair. Other similar incidents had occurred, which William claimed he didn't remember. I believed him because *someone* else was in charge during those moments. Thank God that He puts a hedge of angels around us at times for protection.

Praise God for His promises that assure us we can always depend on help from above in times of distress!

Once more we read the promise of Psalm 91: 11, 12: "For He shall give His angels charge over you, to keep you in all your ways. In their hands they shall bear you up, lest you dash your foot against a stone."

"Fear not, for I am with you; be not dismayed, for I am your God. I will strengthen you, yes, I will help you, I will uphold you with My righteous right hand" (Isa. 41:10).

Was it God's righteous right hand that held on to that chairlift? "My grace is sufficient for you, for My strength is made perfect in weakness" (2 Cor. 12:9).

"In His mercy and faithfulness, God often permits those in whom we place confidence to fail us, in order that we may learn the folly of trusting in man.... Let us trust fully, humbly, unselfishly, in God" (*Gospel Workers,* p. 476).

"Remember, Jesus knows it all—every sorrow, every grief—He will not leave you to sink, for His arms are beneath you" (*Manuscript Releases,* vol. 3, p. 372).

No one who fears God can without danger connect himself with one who fears Him not. "Can two walk together, unless they are agreed" (Amos 3:3).

Chapter Twenty-One

Three Warriors

After one of my annual mammograms, I received a call asking me to return because the results showed some abnormalities. They suggested I needed a needle core biopsy right away. Three years earlier I'd also had this procedure done, so this second time I thought I knew what to expect.

I arrived at the imaging center on time and waited. A lovely, quiet, gentle nurse called me and asked me to follow her to the doctor's office. *Great!* I thought. *He's going to go over the procedure before the biopsy.* But when he spoke, I realized I was in big trouble. He was angrier than a she-bear, yelling at me and at the nurse, "What is she doing here? Get her out of here!"

Shocked and appalled, I just stood there, unable to speak. The nurse tried to calm him down, but he wasn't listening.

"Look at that X-ray," he shouted. "There's nothing wrong with it! Get her out of here. She's wasting my time!" Then he stormed out of the room.

Stunned, I didn't know what to think. Then I rose from my chair and stood really close to the X-ray hanging on the light box on the wall behind me. I looked for what I had seen earlier, when the technician had shown me what was visible after she had enlarged the image by 200 percent. Even I could tell that this was not what I had seen earlier that week. I mentioned this to the nurse, and she immediately left the room. In a short time, she came back. She had arranged for another mammogram to be done right away. It seemed they had misplaced the previous X-ray.

They were not making a good impression here. Once this was completed, I stayed in the waiting room to see what they might decide to do next. I was still in the gown they had provided when the nurse called me back again and said they would begin the needle core biopsy immediately. She then gave me an aspirin for pain. I was starting to get nervous and very anxious right about now.

As I walked into the room where the procedure would take place, I noticed it was a large room with high ceilings and was very dimly lit. The only light I saw was coming from under the table, stationed in one corner of the room, where I would lie during the biopsy. The room seemed so large and empty. The doctor sat in front of a computer-type monitor next to the table. He didn't say a word as we walked in. So his assistant helped me onto the table and instructed me to lie flat on my stomach. I turned my head and lay down my right ear, facing to the left side of my body. Then I heard a sound coming from a motor somewhere underneath me as the table was elevated. I could hear the wheels of the doctor's chair as it rolled right under me, along with his monitor. The nurse would from time to time ask me if I was all right. Her kind and gentle voice was a comfort to me in my anxious state of mind. When everything was set and ready to begin, the doctor said in a gruff voice, "Don't move, or this wand will rip your breast to shreds."

I gasped as I heard these frightful words. *Help!* I thought. *Get me out of here! There's a madman under this table.* I could feel the sting as he inserted the probe. I wanted to flinch every time he removed tissue. But I just lay there, trying hard not to move. There wasn't much cushion on this table, and it felt hard against my face. From time to time, in angry tones, the doctor would remind me to keep still.

Lord, I began to pray in my mind, *help me!* I explained every detail of the situation to Him (as if He didn't already know it) and pled that He would protect me against this horrible doctor. Who knew what he was capable of doing in his angry frame of mind? Almost immediately, I felt calm and noticed that the room, at least toward the ceiling, seemed brighter.

In my mind's eye, I vividly saw three warriors as tall as the room. They were standing with their backs against the wall that was above my head and to the left, in the direction I was facing. Their heads touched the ceiling. Their stature was magnificent. Standing shoulder to shoulder with arms crossed over their chests, their stance was strong and firm. Their legs were spread apart just enough that all three soldiers' feet touched. They were dressed as I imagined the old Roman soldiers would have been: uniforms with a helmet of brass, a brass breastplate, a skirt with metal overlays, and boots with brass coverings reaching up to the knees.

I wondered if I was imagining this or whether these could be mighty angels sent from above in warlike garb, ready to protect. What I heard next astounded me.

"So, Ms. Kennett, do you have any children?" the doctor asked in a calm, gentle voice.

What? I thought. *Is this the same doctor who, just moments before, had shown such contempt toward me?* His whole demeanor had changed in a moment. Much to my amazement, we then carried on a decent and polite conversation that I could hardly believe.

Before long, the procedure was over. The doctor thanked me for being a good patient, then wished me well and said goodbye. *Only God can change a heart like that!* I thought.

This experience reminds me of some precious Bible promises:

"Call to Me, and I will answer you, and show you great and mighty things, which you do not know" (Jer. 33:3).

Stand back; now, this is powerful! "How awesome are Your works! Through the greatness of Your power Your enemies shall submit themselves to You" (Ps. 66:3).

I am almost giddy as I think of how our God protects His children. Yes! He is mighty and powerful and can move mountains out of their place and change the hardness of a human heart in a matter of moments. What an awesome God we serve!

Chapter Twenty-Two

Protected By His Hand

I had been invited to an 80-year-old woman's birthday party. So I went with a few others, and we enjoyed the good food and good company, and we made new elderly friends there.

As the afternoon wore on, one of those in my group began to drink in excess. I believe she was the only one drinking at our table. The alcohol seemed to be fueling something explosive looming deep inside her that could erupt at any time. Soon we decided that it would be best to leave before things got out of control; we could already see some warning signs. We piled into the car and began to drive home, but she was very angry because she didn't want to leave. Then it happened: angry words spewing out of her mouth, directed at those in the front seat. I instinctively knew it wouldn't be long before I might need to have a confrontation with her, because I was sitting next to her in the back seat.

While this was going on, I knew it was only a

matter of time before she would direct her anger at me. I could feel my adrenaline pumping as I tried to figure out how I could defend myself.

I knew it could get physical. I had never been in a fight before, but I could sense it was getting to that point.

So, looking out my side of the window, I began a conversation with my heavenly Father, saying something to the effect of "Lord, when she tries to attack me, I will hold her by the wrists and just hold her there until she calms down." I felt I could do just about anything right about then because I was really on maximum alert and felt incredibly strong at this point. It was the adrenaline taking over.

Soon she called my name and said, "You despicable little worm!" Whew! I turned toward her, called her by her name, and said "You're drunk" Whoops! This just made things worse. Her hands lunged forward with nails like claws coming toward my face. I froze as I looked at her in horror. My hands were paralyzed on my lap as I watched in disbelief while she struggled desperately to claw my face. To my amazement, she could only come within several inches of my face and no farther. She tried and tried, which only made her more angry. Eventually, she gave up and screeched a shrill and dreadful sound, then continued to scream all the way back to our destination.

For the rest of the ride, I felt numb as I sat looking out the window on my side. The only sound we heard were her angry screams of defeat. All the while I thanked God Almighty for His protection. He had put His hand or an angel between the two of us. He saved me from another dreadful incident that could have turned out far worse.

God has promised to protect us: "But the Lord is faithful, who will establish you and guard you from the evil one" (2 Thess. 3:3). (And "the evil one" here is Satan himself, who often works through human beings to hurt us.)

The Scriptures show and tell us that the battle belongs to the Lord. This was proven so clearly to me that day. This battle did belong to the Lord. I was just an innocent bystander.

"He who is in you is greater than he who is in the world" (1 John 4:4).

"For You have armed me with strength for the battle; You have subdued under me those who rose up against me" (Ps. 18:39).

"He hath redeemed my soul in peace from the battle that was against me: for there were many with me" (Ps. 55:18). AMEN.

Chapter Twenty-Three

Just for a Moment

At one point in the middle of winter, it seemed as if I had not seen the sun for many weeks. Every morning I'd leave for work while it was still dark and then also return home in the dark. I never bothered to open the curtains on my windows until the weekend.

Winter just seemed to drain the vitality from my soul. Sitting in a cubicle ten hours a day was taking its toll on me, for the cold or rainy weather had me spend much of my time indoors. So on one particular day, I decided to treat myself to a much-needed massage.

My appointment was immediately after work, so I drove straight there from the office and arrived about 6:30. As I waited alone in the waiting room, I could hear the pouring rain outside. A sense of dread began creeping into my empty soul.

Soon a woman greeted me with a big smile and asked, "Are you Norma?"

I nodded yes.

"Follow me," she said, then led me into a dimly lit room and told me she'd be back in a little while. I got myself ready and climbed onto the table and just relaxed.

My body felt so tired that I seemed to melt right into the bench. A beautiful instrumental CD was playing that I hadn't heard before, so I just lay there, embracing the sounds that calmed my nerves. I must have dozed into a deep sleep, because I seemed to be transported to another place and time.

I found myself sitting in the front of a canoe, softly floating down a river. The sight was beautiful and majestic. Everywhere I looked, it seemed to shimmer and sparkle in beautiful, iridescent colors. Straight, lofty cliffs rose on either side of the river, magnificent to behold as they plummeted to the river's edge. These cliffs were golden in color, and it seemed they were transparent as they shimmered in glorious colors. As I glided along in the canoe, the water also sparkled with similar transparent colors and with the flash of diamonds everywhere I looked. In time I turned and noticed Jesus sitting in the back of the canoe, gently paddling from side to side. I felt I belonged right there with Jesus, ever so near Him in a paradise I couldn't have imagined.

Suddenly, the door opened, and the woman began to ask questions. I shared what I had just experienced and asked her the name of the CD. I believe she said it was "On the Wings of Angels" or something similar.

Appropriate, I thought.

I've noticed more than ever, as I write these little experiences, how often the Lord has comforted me in times of emptiness or when I was overwhelmed with the cares of this life. He is always there.

He has promised, "I will never leave you nor forsake you" (Heb. 13:5). "Yes, I have loved you with an everlasting love; therefore with loving-kindness I have drawn you" (Jer. 31:3).

Also, Ellen G. White has a beautiful statement about how much we matter to God: "Every soul is as fully known to Jesus as if he were the only one for whom the Savior died. The distress of every one touches His heart. The cry for aid reaches His ear" (*The Desire of Ages,* p. 480).

Chapter Twenty-Four

Lifting Boxes

While driving down the mountain from Weimar Institute in the Sierra Foothills after attending a four-day Amazing Facts College of Evangelism seminar, I was telling the Lord I would love to live in the mountains, when I heard a voice say, "Sell your condo and get out of the city. Sell your condo and get out of the city." He said it twice!

Yes, Lord, I thought, *I will. I'll put it on the market right away.*

I had tried to find property or a home in the mountains a couple of years earlier, but after having surgery to remove the tumor in my head, I decided to remain in the city to be close to my doctor a while longer. But now God Himself was commanding me to get out of the city, and I was thrilled at the thought.

Through some friends, I learned of a woman who offered to stage my condo for sale, at no charge. She rearranged my furniture, removed a few things, and using things I already had, she accomplished an amazing and beautiful transformation. *Why didn't I think of that?* I thought to myself. My friend Paul and his team of workers painted my two bathrooms and one wall of the guest room—all because the woman said it would show better—and it did. I had the tile in my kitchen replaced, and the floors in the upstairs bathrooms were also replaced.

John Bridges, a friend of mine, recommended a wonderful woman, Gail Jones, to be my realtor. Before long, she came, took pictures, made a video virtual tour, which she put on the Internet, went over the paperwork, and put up the sign in front. She was very thorough and professional, and I felt I was well taken care of. The neighbors said that it wouldn't sell; apparently, the condo across the street had been on the market for six months and still hadn't sold. "The Lord will sell it," I said. "I'm not concerned." Indeed, I soon had three offers, and it sold in a week—for more than the asking price!

I quickly began to pack and had my large furniture items moved to a storage unit along with some of the many boxes I had already packed. There were still many things I needed to get rid of, and more boxes had to be packed. Earlier I had some help from dear friends from work, and my sister also had come to help me, but now I was on my own. My deadline to move out was critical. Time was running out, and I still had much to do.

But I will never forget one amazing incident. I had just filled a box with books, all Christian books. It contained duplicates of books I had already read, as well as books I hadn't read yet. I had too many books.

So I filled this large box, which was about a foot high, a foot deep, and about five feet long. I didn't tape it shut, as I was just going to drop it off at Goodwill Industries. When it came time to pick up the box to move it, it hit me: *How on earth can I lift all these books? They must weigh a ton,* I thought.

A sense of discouragement filled me. No one was there to help me. I prayed, "Oh, Lord!" and just stood there frozen for a minute. Then I remembered the promise in Philippians 4:13: "I can do all things through Christ who strengthens me." I bent down and grabbed hold of the box, straining for a moment, when suddenly, it became light as a feather. In amazement, I lifted it, walked out of the dining room, past the kitchen, down the walkway to the driveway where my car was parked, and bent over to place it into the trunk.

I stood there for a moment, knowing with all my heart that I'd just had help from above. Maybe it was my guardian angel or the Lord Himself. Still stunned at the thought, I thanked God and continued to fill the car with smaller boxes and other things, all the while reliving the miracle I had just experienced with joy in my heart. The task of moving had taken on a new perspective, knowing as I now did how the Lord was with me in this endeavor. And the move was accomplished by His amazing grace.

Sometimes we wonder how on earth we can accomplish a certain task. We forget that the Lord has a thousand ways to provide what we need of which we know nothing.

"For with God nothing will be impossible" (Luke 1:37).

"And whatever things you ask in prayer, believing, you will receive" (Matt. 21:22).

Jesus says, "You don't have because you don't ask" (James 4:2).

Had I not claimed the promise in Philippians 4:13, I'm not sure God would have sent help. I can't say for sure, but I'm glad this promise came to mind and believed God could answer it His way. This miracle certainly increased my faith in His promises!

Chapter Twenty-Five
Trips to Goodwill

My move from the condo required many trips to Goodwill. I'll share now two different memories of that time, which are still very dear and clear in my mind.

At this point in my move, I was feeling pretty overwhelmed and exhausted. Packing boxes, running up and down stairs, driving back and forth to Goodwill, hardly taking the time to eat—all this was wearing me down. The process would begin from the moment I got up in the morning and continue until I went to bed. Time was running out, and the new owner wanted to move in as soon as possible. Since the moving company had already moved my furniture into a storage unit, I was sleeping in my sleeping bag on the dining room floor.

When I first moved into this condo, I knew it was an answer to prayer and thought I would never move again. Yet here I was, because of God's command and my willingness to move out of the city and into the mountains (this was a lifelong dream for me).

On one of these evenings, I recalled some memories of my time in this condo. It was in this dining room that I had written out my last will and testament. In my bedroom, I had poured out my heart and emptied myself, surrendering my all so that God's will would be done in my life. Here in this place, I had heard the Lord speak my name and reveal to me the meaning of the dream I'd had in surgery. Here, too, God filled the emptiness of my soul to overflowing, and I'd never be the same again. For the first year I lived here, I would get up every night and sit on the step of the sunken living room and thank God for this lovely home, which I never felt worthy to own. This was a home of overwhelming joy and overwhelming trials that led me to a stronger faith in the God of Heaven.

Morning came, and I was up and at it again. I was making yet another trip to Goodwill. It's amazing how quickly you can accumulate stuff in a span of just nine years! As I pulled into the back parking lot of Goodwill, a young man came over as I opened the trunk of the car.

"Hi," I said. "Could you place this box of books in the correct bin for me?"

He looked into the open box filled with Christian books and just stared, seeming not even to hear me. Then he spoke two words: "New Testament?" His question took me by surprise.

"Are you a Christian?" I asked.

"Yes," he replied.

"Oh, I don't have a Bible with me right now," I told him. "But I need to make another trip, and I'll bring one for you when I return." He seemed happy.

"Go get yourself a bag," I said. When he returned, I began to fill it with books I felt would be a blessing to him. He emptied the car, and I left for another load.

I returned with a Bible I had never used. Often I had wondered why I hadn't felt impressed to use it. Now I knew it was so I could give it away. This young man came quickly to the car, and I gave him the Bible along with my extra set of the Bible on CD. After he emptied the car, we spoke for a moment.

"What's your name?" I asked.

"Jacob."

"Ah," I said, "that's a good name. It's in the Bible!"

He nodded with a big smile, as if to say, "I know."

On another trip to Goodwill later that same week, I had another box, much the same size as before, also filled with books and two copies of the *Final Events* DVDs by Amazing Facts on top. I had meant to take those out but forgot to remove them from the box until I opened the trunk. Just then another young man walked over and stood next to me, staring at the box of books. As I asked him to take the box, I picked up the two DVDs lying on top and noticed that his eyes were riveted on them.

"Do you want a DVD?" I asked. Without saying a word, he nodded quickly, his eyes open wide. I gave him one, but he continued to stare at the other DVD too, so I asked, "Do you want this one too?"

"Yes!" he responded. So I gave him the other one also.

"Are you a Christian?" I asked.

"Yes!" he replied.

"Then go get yourself a bag, and let's fill it for you." He eagerly returned with a bag, and I began to fill it with books such as *Bible Studies for the Home* and others that I thought would be good reading. He emptied the car for me, then came to the trunk, which he saved for last, and set the large box on the ground.

"What's your name?" I asked.

"Gabriel!" he said. "It's in the Bible!"

"Yes it is!" I replied, and we both just stood there a moment with a joy that seemed to say we both loved Jesus. As I said goodbye and drove away, I looked in my rearview mirror and saw him taking more books out of the box, filling his bag to the brim.

We never know when we might have a divine appointment that the Lord has already arranged for us beforehand. I was glad that I just so happened to have ample material to give away. I prayed that these two young men would, as a result, have a closer relationship with their Savior and that, when I get to heaven, I will see them there and be able to hear their stories.

Chapter Twenty-Six

Homeless Man

I had just left my new friend Gabriel from Goodwill Industries. On this particular day, I realized I hadn't had anything to eat, except for my green drink early that morning. Now it was about 4:15 in the afternoon, and I still had much to do, but I decided to get something quickly. Chipotle Mexican Grill seemed to be my best bet, as it was close to my home. I figured I would get a burrito to take home and then rest awhile.

As I sat in my car waiting for the light to turn green so I could make a left-hand turn, I noticed a homeless man sitting on the corner in front of the bank across the street from Chipotle. I had noticed him there earlier that summer but had never felt impressed to help him. I have helped homeless people before, sometimes because of compassion and other times because I have felt impressed. I try not to let those feeling pass without acting on them.

I remembered seeing him earlier that summer in a heavy, faded-green army jacket as he sat on the ground with his legs up against his chest and his arms around his knees and his head facing down as if trying to keep the light of day out of his eyes. I wondered how he was able to sit there in those heavy clothes in the heat of the day given the temperatures of 105 degrees Fahrenheit at times. As I sat there contemplating who he might be and where he might have come from, I suddenly had an overwhelming impulse to feed him. I was so overcome by this impression that it brought me to tears (I had never experienced this before). My heart began to race as I prayed, "Lord, please keep him there until I can offer him something to eat. And when I approach him on that side of the street, please let the light stay red, so I can hand him the food."

Standing in line at Chipotle was very intense for me, as I feared he might leave. I quickly ordered two meals. I thought twice about adding guacamole to his burrito but added a bottle of cold water and put a five-dollar bill in his bag, praying all the while that he would still be there.

By God's grace, there he was, still sitting with his head down and his arms blanketing the outer edge of his face. I thanked God that the light was red and that no cars were behind me. I pulled up to the curve that only made a right-hand turn. Then I rolled my window all the way down and called out, "Sir?"

He didn't budge, so louder, I almost shouted, "Hello, Sir?"

He lifted his head ever so slowly. His hair was a dirty-brown color that almost blended with his faded, dirty-green army jacket. I noticed he had a receding hairline. He had difficulty getting to his feet. Then, sort of hunched over, he slowly walked to my car. Since my window was rolled all the way down on the passenger side, he put his head inside the car and just stared at me.

When I saw him up close, I was startled. He had a most beautiful face: clear blue eyes, jet-black brows, the longest eyelashes I had ever seen, a jet-black mustache, and a short-trimmed beard around his chin. I noticed that the hair around his face was also jet-black, yet the rest of it was brown. As I studied his beautiful face, I noticed that his hairline almost appeared to be in front of another face, almost as if they weren't attached. It seemed as if I saw movement between the two; it's hard to describe.

He just looked so calm and beautiful, just staring back into my eyes. I finally got my wits about me and handed him the bag and said with a shaky voice, almost stuttering, "There's a bu-bu-burrito, and bo-bo-bottled water and a fi-fi-five-dollar bill in the bag." He took it and just continued to stare at me for a moment.

"God loves you," I said. I can't remember whether he replied at all. Then he slowly backed out from the window and walked slowly to his spot on the corner. As he walked away, I noticed his hair now seemed to be brown all over. I couldn't seem to put it all together.

Amazingly, the light just then turned green, and I drove away. I don't know how long it took to turn green, but it seemed quite a while. I was emotionally affected to tears. As I drove home, I asked, "Lord, was that an angel? Was that *my* angel? Was that *You,* Lord?"

I continued talking to God: "I hate the evil one who deceives poor souls to the depths of homelessness. He tempts them to think that his ways are satisfying and more exciting, only to leave people empty and demoralized, with nothing but hopelessness and needing to depend on the mercy of others for a handout of food or money." At that moment, I was angry at the evil one for his deceptions, for I seemed to see them in a new light. Then a thought came to mind: *I wish I had put guacamole on his burrito!*

When I arrived home about five minutes later, I put my burrito down and paced the floor in my empty condo, still deeply moved about the whole incident. I wondered if this was from above. If it was, I felt unworthy And if it wasn't, I still longed to be ever closer to Jesus. All I know is that I came away from this experience changed in some way.

These were days of physical and emotional testing for me. I was exhausted from the move, even though I was excited and thankful for it. I was depleted and overwhelmed by all the work that still needed to be done so quickly. My time to move was running out, the minutes were constantly at my heels, and I felt I could not rest until it was all done.

Yet as I looked back, I could see that God was with me all along the way, showering me with blessings along and helping me lift the burden of all those boxes—as well as leading me to meet two brothers in Christ. Then He refreshed me with His goodness through sharing a burrito, possibly with an angel!

The Bible has these words for us: "Do not forget to entertain strangers, for by doing so some have unwittingly entertained angels" (Heb. 13:2).

Jesus says: For I was hungry and you gave Me food; I was thirsty and you gave Me drink; I was a stranger and you took Me in; I was naked and you clothed Me; I was sick and you visited Me; I was in prison and you came to Me.... Assuredly, I say to you, inasmuch as you did it to one of the least of these My brethren, you did it to Me (Matt. 25:35, 36, 40).

Closing Thoughts

Have you had times in your life when you felt broken because your earthly father didn't keep his promises or was emotionally or physically abusive? Or perhaps he neglected you, abandoned you, or made you feel you could never measure up to his expectations? Did you always seem to fail in every effort to win his affection?

During those times your compassionate heavenly Father was there with you. Everything you experienced was written in the books of heaven. He saw and felt your pain, the disappointments and tears; He wept with you. Reach out and claim Him as your very own heavenly Father.

"He relieves the fatherless and widow" (Ps. 146:9).

"You are the helper of the fatherless" (Ps. 10:14).

"A father of the fatherless, and a defender of the widows, is God in His holy habitation" (Ps. 68:5).

Ladies, have you been neglected by your earthly husband? Has he broken promises and left you for someone else? Has he been unfaithful or abusive? Jesus saw it all and understands, and He has never left your side. Has your husband died, and now you find yourself alone? Choose Jesus as your heavenly husband as I have. He has never broken a promise or left my side for one minute. Remember His promises.

"For your Maker is your husband, the Lord of hosts is His name; and your Redeemer is the Holy One of Israel; He is called the God of the whole earth. For the Lord has called you like a woman forsaken and grieved in spirit, like a youthful wife when you were refused: says your God" (Isa. 54:5, 6).

He loves you so much that your name is on the palms of His hands, and He remembers your tears: "See, I have inscribed you on the palms of My hands" (Isa. 49:16).

"You number my wanderings; put my tears into Your bottle; are they not in Your book?" (Ps. 56:8).

Some final thoughts from childhood: I knew there was a God. But He always felt bigger than my little mind could imagine. But as the years flew by, and I experienced trials of all sizes, shapes, and colors, I now see that Jesus was always there. So much turmoil, pain and sorrow exists in this world. It doesn't look as if that's about to change. But what we can hold on to is knowing that Jesus, our Burden Bearer, sees it all. He feels our woes and sorrows and weeps with us.

The Bible is filled with prophecies showing that Jesus is about to return. Soon He will come and take to heaven those who love and obey Him, because they long to be with Him. What I have shared is one person's heartaches, trials, and joys. I wouldn't change a thing. If this is what it has taken for me to know my heavenly Father as closely as I do now, then so be it.

If you don't have a close relationship with the God of heaven, the God of the universe, I encourage you to make time to read your Bible and get to know Him as your lifeline to heaven. Soon you will begin to notice a change come over you that will draw you closer and closer to the source of love—the One who stretched out His arms on the cross of Calvary, who bled and died and took our sins upon Himself. As He took time to die for us that we might have eternal life, we should take time to get to know Him through His word.

The Bible promises, "Draw near to God and He will draw near to you" (James 4:8).

And once you have developed that relationship with God, don't let anything else stand between the two of you. Nothing can compare to His matchless, incomprehensible divine love. It's yours at no expense to you, paid by the high cost of His precious blood, which is worth more than gold or silver or anything this world can offer. All that we see around us will perish one day. Jesus promises eternal life and joy that is indescribable. Don't miss out on the most amazing gift ever offered to mankind. You can't find it anywhere else.

Remember, "not in freedom from trials, but in the midst of it, is Christian character developed. Exposure to rebuffs and opposition leads the follower of Christ to greater watchfulness and more earnest prayer to the mighty Helper. Severe trials endured by the grace of God develops patience, vigilance, fortitude, and a deep and abiding trust in God" (*The Acts of the Apostles*, pp. 467, 468).

"By living faith you are to trust Him, even though the impulse is strong within you to speak words of distrust" (*Testimonies to Ministers and Gospel Workers*, p. 517). Paul wrote in 2 Corinthians 5:7 that "we walk by faith, not by sight."

I would like to share a comment from Ellen White that has melted my very soul and has brought incredible hope and assurance:

> Through all our trials we have a never failing Helper. He does not leave us alone to struggle with temptation, to battle with evil, and be finally crushed with burdens and sorrow. Though now He is hidden from mortal sight, the ear of faith can hear His voice saying, Fear not; I am with you. "I am He that liveth, and was dead; and, behold, I am alive forevermore." Revelation 1:18. I have endured your sorrows, experienced your struggles, encountered your temptations. I know your tears; I also have wept. The griefs that lie too deep to be breathed into any human ear, I know. Think not that you are desolate and forsaken. Though your pains touch no responsive chord in any heart on earth, look unto Me, and live. "The mountains shall depart, and the hills be removed; but My kindness shall not depart from thee, neither shall the covenant

of My peace be removed, saith the Lord that hath mercy on thee." Isaiah 54:10. (*The Desire of Ages*, p.483)

Each day is a gift from above. Our lives here on earth are nothing but a whisper, compared to eternity. Live each day as if it's your last, and let the love of Jesus shine through.

At the moment I am in the mist of another challenge of illness that, if nothing were to change, could take my life in the not-too-distant future. Yet, I have the assurance that I am in the palms of God's hands. It was His hands that created the universe and made man in His image. It was his hands that were nailed to the cross on Calvary. Therefore, I have surrendered my will knowing that He knows what is best for my eternal good. In my heart there is a joy that keeps me content, even when the future seems uncertain. He will continue to be my Stronghold. For no one has ever loved me like Jesus.

I AM means an eternal presence; the past, present, and future are alike to God. He sees the most remote events of past history and the far distant with as clear a vision as we do those things that are transpiring daily. We know not what is before us, and if we did it would not contribute to our eternal welfare. God gives us an opportunity to exercise faith and trust in the great I AM. (*Manuscript Releases*, vol. 14, 1895)

In closing, I want to share one final thought.

> Live in contact with the living Christ, and
> He will hold you firmly by a hand that will
> never let go. Know and believe the love
> that God has to us, and you are secure;
> that love is a fortress impregnable to all
> the delusions and assaults of Satan. "The
> name of the Lord is a strong tower: the
> righteous runneth into it, and is safe."
> Proverbs 18:10. (*Thoughts from the Mount
> of Blessing,* p. 119)

Reader Reviews

"In this book Norma Kennett takes the various dark shadows of her life and strokes them onto the bright page of God's compassion. Out of these suffering shadows emerges a portrait of comfort, hope, and the real purpose and a definite meaning for life."

—Pastor Robert Ross

"Sharing this author's deep, heartfelt experience from cover to cover has given me a greater sense of God's personal presence in our lives, no matter where we are on life's journey—and hence brings courage and comfort for the road ahead."

—Esmé Ross

"Are you longing for a more intimate relationship with Jesus? Read Norma's thrilling story!"

—Mary Morris, friend

"Norma's riveting story proves once again that God's grace is sufficient to help us meet any challenge or walk through any dark valley."

—Ken McFarland

"Norma Kennett's story reveals a picture of our loving, caring God. On every page she reminds us that God hears and answers prayer, sometimes in the most dramatic ways. You will be blessed by reading this book."

—Ricardo B. Graham, President, Pacific Union Conference of Seventh-day Adventists

We invite you to view the complete
selection of titles we publish at:

www.TEACHServices.com

Scan with your mobile
device to go directly
to our website.

Please write or email us your praises, reactions, or
thoughts about this or any other book we publish at:

TEACH Services, Inc.
P U B L I S H I N G
www.TEACHServices.com • (800) 367-1844

P.O. Box 954
Ringgold, GA 30736

info@TEACHServices.com

TEACH Services, Inc., titles may be purchased in bulk for
educational, business, fund-raising, or sales promotional use.
For information, please e-mail:

BulkSales@TEACHServices.com

Finally, if you are interested in seeing
your own book in print, please contact us at

publishing@TEACHServices.com

We would be happy to review your manuscript for free.

CPSIA information can be obtained
at www.ICGtesting.com
Printed in the USA
FFOW01n0057240617
37011FF

9 781479 601264